"Melanie McNally has gifted teens, and the adults who love them, with a powerful resource to begin creating a life they'll love. Her expert knowledge of how to manage the real challenges young people face shines through on every page. Readers will love *The Emotionally Intelligent Teen* for its clear introduction to the language of emotional intelligence, and exercises that empower teens to try on new mental health skills."

—**Chanel Dokun,** cofounder of Healthy Minds NYC, and author of *Life Starts Now*

"Melanie McNally's book is a groundbreaking lifeline for teens and their unique struggles. She connects with the reader using easily accessible language and compelling case examples. McNally makes abstract concepts clear, and offers an arsenal of helpful tools. I highly recommend *The Emotionally Intelligent Teen.*"

—**Larry Maucieri, PhD, ABPP-CN,** board-certified clinical neuropsychologist, and coeditor of *The Distracted Couple*

"McNally's book creatively provides hands-on tools that teens can easily learn, practice, and apply in everyday interactions with peers, family, and self! More than ever, teens need these skills to learn to 'go deeper' versus 'coasting' as she describes, allowing them to grow into emotionally intelligent adults. Teens will develop self-awareness, mindfulness, and self-regulation skills through interactive journal entries and 'vibe checks.' This book should be on every teen's shelf!"

—**Kristen Markovich, PsyD,** clinical psychologist, and private practice owner in Schaumburg, IL

"Teens today are under a high degree of pressure and stress, this book will give you the tools to feel satisfied with life, while embracing your emotional responses to life's ups and downs. *The Emotionally Intelligent Teen* is a masterclass in training your mind, providing useful strategies and thought-provoking prompts to increase mental health and resiliency. Through the book's daily practice and reflection, you will create healthy mind habits."

—**Stacie M. Herrera, PsyD,** owner of Herrera Psychology, cofounder of HumanizEDU, and coauthor of *Unpacking Bliss*

the **emotionally intelligent teen**

skills to **help you deal** with **what you feel, build stronger relationships** & **boost self-confidence**

MELANIE MCNALLY, PsyD

Instant Help Books
An Imprint of New Harbinger Publications, Inc.

Publisher's Note

NEW HARBINGER PUBLICATIONS is a registered trademark of New Harbinger Publications, Inc.

New Harbinger Publications is an employee-owned company.

New Harbinger Publications, Inc.
5720 Shattuck Avenue
Oakland, CA 94609
www.newharbinger.com

Cover design by Amy Shoup

Acquired by Jennye Garibaldi

Edited by Karen Schader

FSC
www.fsc.org
MIX
Paper from
responsible sources
FSC® C011935

Library of Congress Cataloging-in-Publication Data on file

Printed in the United States of America

25   24   23

10   9   8   7   6   5   4   3   2   1   First Printing

For Sean, I love doing life with you.

Contents

Overview

Welcome! I'm so glad you're here. It's not always easy to decide to work on ourselves, and the fact that you're reading this right now says so much about you. I'm guessing that you're a strong person who's interested in personal growth. I bet that you don't see yourself as brave, but others do. And that you're someone who doesn't run from a challenge. You're someone who wants to feel different but doesn't quite know what to do. I'm also guessing that you might be like most teens who feel misunderstood and have problems with relationships. Perhaps, like so many people, you get upset easily and become overwhelmed with emotions. And just like most of us, you don't want to blow up easily, fight with your family or friends, or worry constantly, but really don't know how else to manage your feelings.

Well, you, my friend, have made a good choice. You want to learn how to feel better. You want to improve your relationships. You want to make different choices. You want to improve and like yourself. And you've chosen to do something about it. That's huge! The very fact that you picked up this book and are now reading it says that you're capable of creating the change you want. It says that you have the drive and desire that will motivate you to do the work. You're reading this for a reason and, together, we're going to learn how to recognize your feelings so you can manage them better, which will lead you to better relationships and choices. We're going to do a lot of work in this book, and you're going to come out the other side with a better understanding of yourself and others and with lots of tools in your emotional toolkit.

Before we get started, let's just get something out of the way. This book will help only if you're willing to do the work. I'll give you the information, examples, and lessons; however, it's up to you to take the time to absorb and think about it all. I'll provide the exercises, journal prompts, reflection questions, and tools; however, it's up to you to use them. This book won't do much for you if you only passively read it. You're going to have to actively engage with it. You're going to have to do more than just read the words, you'll have to think of how each section applies to your own life, take time to journal, and actually do the exercises so you get to practice what you're learning.

It's kind of like in school—how you perform better on tests when you use more active forms of studying, like attending study groups, watching videos on the content, talking about the material with your peers, or drawing diagrams or maps to better understand connections and timelines. You know how sometimes you skip all those things and just reread the text and notes, go through flash cards mindlessly, and then wonder why you didn't do as well as usual? It's because rereading is a passive form of studying, and our brains do much better when we study and learn in the more active ways of study groups, videos, talking, and drawing mentioned above. If you want to get the most you can out of this book, engage with it in an active way, not a passive way.

To actively engage with this book means to pause and reflect on sentences or paragraphs so you can think about how it applies to your own life. It means to underline or highlight things that stand out to you (only if you own the book! Please don't do that it if it's borrowed!). It also means to have your own personal journal next to you when reading to take notes, answer reflection questions, and respond to journal prompts. There will be exercises and tools included in each chapter, so make sure you try each one out! You'll get so much more out of this book and will create the change you're looking for if you do these things.

What Is Emotional Intelligence?

Emotional intelligence is the ability to notice one's own and other people's emotions, to be able to tell the difference between emotions and label them appropriately, and to use emotional information to guide thinking and behavior (A *Dictionary of Psychology*, 3rd ed., s.v. "emotional intelligence"). Emotional intelligence is made up of three components—emotional awareness, self-regulation, and interpersonal skills. To understand what it means to have emotional intelligence, let's first define each component. *Emotional awareness* is the ability to understand emotions (our own and others'), for example, knowing when you're feeling frustrated or recognizing when someone else is feeling disappointed. *Self-regulation* is the ability to manage your emotions and behaviors, like being able to walk away from someone when you're really angry instead of screaming at them. *Interpersonal skills* are the healthy, productive ways you interact and communicate with others, such as putting down your phone to show you're listening or asking questions to demonstrate interest in what someone else is saying.

It sounds like a lot and can be overwhelming to think about all at once. But this book is going to break it down and teach you step by step. You will build the skills you'll need to be more aware—and in control—of your emotions so that you can have healthy relationships with others. Isn't that what we all need? Wouldn't the world be a better place if everyone had these skills? Just imagine a school, job, friend group, or family where everyone understood their own emotions better (emotional awareness) and knew how to manage their intense feelings (self-regulation). And imagine that this same group understood how others might be feeling (emotional awareness) and people were able to offer empathy or guidance when needed (interpersonal skills). Wouldn't the group you imagined function differently than they do now? Wouldn't you feel different about spending time with them?

Learning emotional intelligence is a big job and, unfortunately, not something that's taught in every school. (Imagine if it was! What a different world it would be if emotional intelligence was a subject in school, just like history, math, or science.) Being emotionally intelligent doesn't just come with age either; it's something that we must consciously learn and work on. There are a whole lot of adults out there lacking emotional intelligence—just think of the adults in your own life. I'm sure you can name one or two who don't really seem to understand their own feelings or the feelings of others, who are constantly in conflict with others, and who don't have control over their emotions much of the time. But you're going to be different and in a much better spot to manage life because you're learning it now. No matter where you fall on the emotional-intelligence spectrum, from lacking all the skills to needing improvement in some areas, you're going to learn and grow.

We already learned the components that make up emotional intelligence—emotional awareness, self-regulation, and interpersonal skills. In this book, we're going to break these components down further so that you have a strong foundation to build upon. We're going to focus on the foundational skills of emotional intelligence, the building blocks that are essential to our emotional health. These foundational skills include self-awareness of emotions, thoughts, and behaviors; understanding physical sensations; awareness of others; and self-regulation. Once we're able to use these foundational skills well, we're in a good spot to create goals that are truly aligned with what we feel, we're better able to communicate our feelings and needs, and we can manage our own hard feelings, like stress, anxiety, and depression, much better than before.

Becoming more emotionally intelligent involves multiple steps and lots of work. We don't just memorize the steps and then, voilà, we're emotionally aware, in control, and done. If only it were that easy! No, we must learn the steps and then implement them day in and day out. We must practice, talk through, journal, and work on the steps over and over until we start noticing change. And then we keep working. Because it's not something we learn and finish. It's an ongoing process that we work on all our lives.

The Importance of Emotions

Emotions impact everything. How we feel impacts everything. And I mean everything. You think I'm exaggerating? Let's take a closer look.

Danika is a sixteen-year-old high schooler who awoke this morning to her parents arguing. She pulls herself out of bed thinking that her parents' argument means they're divorcing, just like her friend's parents who constantly fought before finally getting a divorce. She isn't noticing how this thought makes her feel, but instead realizes that her stomach hurts a bit. She doesn't want to upset her stomach further, so she decides to skip breakfast. She barely acknowledges her mom in the kitchen as she makes her lunch for school and then leaves. As she pulls into the school parking lot, she finally notices how she's feeling: irritated. She's irritated by having to park so far away from the main doors, irritated by all the smiling faces, irritated that her stomach is growling, and irritated that she forgot an assignment at home. When she runs into a few friends near her locker, they jokingly comment on how she's late yet again, which causes her irritation to bubble over into snapping at them. They tell her she needs to learn how to take a joke and chill, and they walk away, leaving her feeling even worse than before.

Danika's emotions affected everything. You might be thinking, *It's not her emotions that affected everything, it's the circumstances that ruined her morning.* It was her parents fighting, having to park far away, being hungry, and her friends teasing her. We'll break down Danika's story a bit in just a moment and see if you think differently.

Emotions are part of your life whether you're aware of them or not. They're part of the human experience. Emotions can be positive or negative, and what's more, what we do with our feelings can have positive or negative consequences. The consequence part is usually the area we focus on, not the feelings that caused the behavior that led to the consequence. We're going to focus on awareness of emotions *and* awareness of behaviors in this book so that you learn how to separate feelings and behaviors.

Let's consider Danika's story again. What if she had been working on becoming more emotionally intelligent? How might her morning have changed?

What if Danika had taken a pause to consider how she felt (self-awareness of emotions) and what she was thinking (self-awareness of thoughts) when she awoke to her parents' argument? What if she noticed how her body was reacting and knew what those sensations meant (understanding physical sensations)? What if her self-awareness caused her to do something about her negative feelings (self-regulation)? Let's change her story to reflect that process:

Danika is a sixteen—year—old high schooler who awoke this morning to her parents arguing. She takes a moment to notice that her body feels tense—her jaw is clenched and her shoulders are pulled up toward her ears. She realizes that this tension means she's feeling anxious. She also notices that she's thinking that her parents have been arguing a lot lately, that her friend's parents argued all the time and they divorced, and that she's wondering if her parents might also divorce. She decides to take a couple of slow deep breaths, she tells herself that she's safe and that her parents' argument doesn't mean they're divorcing, and she gets out of bed. She notices that she's still a little anxious but not as bad as a few moments earlier.

These simple acts of self-awareness and self-regulation will likely change Danika's entire morning. She's now feeling more relaxed and can eat breakfast, which will decrease her irritability. What if she also notices how a parent is feeling (awareness of others' emotions)? Let's see if that changes anything else for her.

Danika enters the kitchen to grab breakfast and make her lunch for the day. She sees her mom sitting hunched over at the table, staring into her coffee cup. Danika recognizes her mom's posture and body language and thinks her mom might be feeling hurt. She asks, "Are you okay, Mom? Can I sit with you?" Her mom notices Danika and smiles. "That's sweet of you, honey. I'm okay. Dad and I just can't seem to agree on a big financial decision, and it's stressful. We'll figure it out eventually, but it just feels really hard right now." Danika feels relief in knowing more about their argument and hearing her mom's perspective. She sits down with her to eat her cereal, and they talk about the huge thunderstorm that shook the house the night before.

Danika is likely to feel less stressed and anxious leaving the house now that she knows what the argument was about and isn't worrying about her parents divorcing. She might even play her favorite song as she drives to school, which will make her care less about having to park far away and to feel less irritated in general. Her mood will be completely different when she approaches her friends, and their teasing might make her smile instead of snarl.

She started off with self-awareness of her feelings, thoughts, and physical sensations, used a self-regulation tool to feel less anxious, and was considerate of her mom's feelings. By using some of the skills that you'll learn in this book, her morning completely changed.

How This Work Changes You

Adolescence and young adulthood are full of ups and downs. You get to be more independent but also have more responsibility. You get to try new and challenging activities, but you also experience more demanding environments and situations. You get to enter romantic relationships, but you also must manage new interpersonal skills. You get to make more choices without your parents or family's input, but you also face harsher consequences. Given the new dynamics you're facing as a teen or young adult, becoming more self-aware is crucial so that you learn how to manage hard emotions and thoughts, have better control over your actions, and can move through relationships successfully (Young, Sandman, and Craske 2019). In other words, things are changing all around you and that can be extremely stressful; however, if you're aware of how you're feeling and thinking, you'll be better able to manage your behaviors, reactions, and relationships.

Besides all these ups and downs, there's a lot of development happening inside your body and brain right now. Puberty-related changes to hormones, bodies, and brains start during adolescence and continue into young adulthood. Additionally, your brain is creating new neural connections, which affect decision making, learning, and social interactions (Laube, van den Bos, and Fandakova 2020). All this change and development means that you're growing, maturing, and evolving at a rapid rate during this period. It can feel disorienting and perhaps scary as you notice new ways of thinking and how your preferences change quickly. Maybe you used to love playing the piano in front of others but now find that you don't. Or the friend group you were so close to last semester now feels like strangers. These changes are normal, and while it might feel like you have no idea who you are sometimes, this is exactly how you're figuring out who you are. These changes to identity and preferences are to be expected and demonstrate that you're growing and adapting.

Your brain is working hard to continue its growth too, kind of like how your bones and muscles continue to get stronger. You know how the more you exercise and eat well, the stronger you get? Well, the more you learn, the stronger your brain gets. And just like our bodies benefit from vaccines to fight off illnesses and protect our physical health, there are things we can do to protect our brains and mental health. A group of Australian researchers found that there are essential habits that teens and young adults need to foster this growth and development. They call these habits a "mental vaccine" because practicing them helps boost your growth and provides conditions for the greatest brain improvements. The habits that make up their vaccine include healthy eating, exercise, rest and sleep, optimism, managing stress, making autonomous decisions, variety and challenge, social interactions with friends, learning new things, and repetition (Ekman et al. 2021). While we won't be diving into each of these items, you'll likely recognize some of these habits in the exercises, reflections, and goal setting that you'll be doing here.

You're at an important period of development right now, whether you've just started adolescence or are wrapping it up in young adulthood. Your brain is ready for growth—it's primed for it right now! It's ready to make new connections and pathways, ready to think differently, and ready to make positive change. When you do the work involved in this book, your brain will respond by adapting and growing in a positive direction. You can and will feel, think, and behave differently, which will in turn change how you interact with others. This is possible at any stage of life; however, it's the most doable at the phase you're in right now. I honestly can't think of a more important thing to be doing.

How to Use This Book

Understanding our own emotions and the emotions of others well enough to be able to set and achieve goals, communicate our needs and feelings, and have healthy relationships is a lot to do in one book. However, you'll see how all these things go together and build upon one another. Take your time and go at your own pace. We're in no hurry. It's more important that you learn these steps than that you get through this book by a certain date. If that means you spend more time on one chapter than another, that's totally fine. And if it also means that you take your time on journal prompts or exercises before moving on so that you have extra time for reflections or skill building, that's great. You're learning in your way and on your timeline.

You'll notice that within the chapters are exercises for reflection and practice. Sometimes you'll be asked to grab your journal and respond to questions or prompts. Those are good spots to really pause and think about what you're learning and how it applies to your own life. There are also sections that provide step-by-step directions so that you can work on what you've learned in the real world. Additionally, you'll notice "vibe checks" later in the book. Vibe checks are there to help you stay on track with the goals you'll set during chapter 4 and are a chance to reflect on your progress.

Coasting and Getting Stuck

Learning new things can be difficult, and getting stuck is to be expected. If you're not being challenged to think differently, then you're not truly learning, are you? Think about a class you've taken where you barely had to pay attention and aced all your tests and assignments. Did you really learn anything in that class, or were you just going through the motions of learning? If you find this happening sometimes in this book, if you realize you're coasting and not really paying attention because you're already familiar with the concepts, I suggest using that time as an opportunity to go deeper.

Sydney is bored out of her mind in her culinary arts class. She attended a specialized camp last summer for aspiring chefs where she spent two weeks creating complex menus, cooking elaborate meals, and working with a team of seasoned chefs. When her high school teacher assigns the project of cooking your favorite meal, she groans with boredom and wonders why they couldn't do something a litter harder. When she complains to her parents over dinner about the lack of creativity in this assignment, her mom suggests that she turn it into something more. Sydney considers this idea and, later that night, sits down and brainstorms until she comes up with something she'd be proud to share with the seasoned chefs from camp. When the day comes to present her favorite meal, instead of cooking it ahead of time and putting it on a plate in front of her teacher like each of her peers does, she dims the lights, plays music, and walks her entire class through how to cook the meal from start to finish all the while sharing stories about why she loves this meal and what each ingredient means to her.

Sydney chose to go deeper rather than to coast. Going deeper in this book means pausing and reflecting on how something applies to you, even if you think you've already mastered the area. Think about yourself in different contexts and situations, and with different people around. How might the material apply then? Going deeper also means checking in with others to see if your perception of yourself aligns with others' perceptions of you. For instance, you may think you're great at noticing how others feel and don't really need to spend much time on this area. You may think you're an incredible listener and understand social cues really well. Ask some trusted family members and friends for an honest assessment. Ask them if they feel heard when in conversations with you. See if they feel like you understand when they're upset and why.

Or perhaps you think you manage your feelings well and don't need to practice new self-regulation tools. Check in with a parent, coach, friend, or teacher, and ask them if they notice when you're frustrated, irritated, or overwhelmed. How do they observe you handling those tough feelings, and what do they think you need to work on?

Now think of a class that drove you bananas. Where you had to meet with a tutor, attend study groups, see the teacher during office hours for questions, or wanted to pull your hair out. What did you end up learning in that class? After you scream "Nothing!" take another look. I bet you learned some things in that class that are still with you today. Perhaps physics made sense in college because of that challenging high school class. Or maybe you realized you're a really hard worker and can succeed when you put in effort because of the music class you struggled through in middle school.

Paul feels stuck in his geometry class and is beginning to think he'll never be able to major in engineering in college like he planned. As he sits down with a friend to study for an upcoming test, he notices how fidgety his body feels and how irritated he is by his friend's gum chewing. He begins thinking, *I'll never get this*, and *I should just find something else to major in at college that doesn't involve math*. When he gets up to use the library bathroom, he catches his reflection in the mirror and realizes how irritated and fidgety he feels and that he's thinking negative and unhelpful thoughts. He knows he needs to do something different or he isn't going to break this cycle. When he sits back down at the table, he goes back to the chapter his class just finished rather than starting on the new assigned one. He decides that he'll keep going back in his book, mastering each concept that's confusing, until he finds a section that makes perfect sense. And that's how he spends his Saturday—reading and reworking each previous section until he fully understands it, and stopping when he reaches material that is easy. By Saturday evening he feels better about geometry and needs a break. He invites friends over for a bonfire and s'mores.

Paul recognized he was stuck, backed up, and then took a break. Getting stuck might occur when you feel challenged in such a way that you have no idea what to do. It can be hard to recognize in the moment, so it's important that you know your signs of being stuck.

Like Paul, many people know they're stuck when they feel fidgety or need to get up and move their body somehow, like pacing or cleaning. They also might notice that they're irritated with the material, the author of the material, or the person teaching them the material. Some people even become irritated with themselves when they're stuck and, like Paul, engage in negative or harmful self-talk; for example, *I'm so stupid*, or *I'll never learn this*, or *What's the point of getting this? It's not going to help me anyway.*

Self-talk is defined as "statements, phrases, or cue words that are addressed to the self which might be said automatically or strategically, either out loud or silently, phrased positively or negatively, having an instructional or motivational purpose, an element of interpretation, and incorporating some of the same grammatical features associated with everyday speech" (Hardy and Zourbanos 2016). Essentially, if your thought is directed at you, it's self-talk.

Grab your journal and take a moment to reflect. What are your signs of being stuck?

Once you know these signs, you can do what Paul did and back up. He reread and reworked each previous concept until it clicked. Often, we're stuck on something new because we haven't fully understood the previous lesson. In this book, if you find that the previous lesson didn't really click, go back a section. It's important that you're understanding what you're reading as you go; otherwise you might end up lost and frustrated. Keep going back until you find an area that makes total sense. Now you're at a familiar place and can build from there after taking a break.

Taking a break is when we step away from the material to clear our minds. Have you ever noticed how things make sense after a break? I know I've had times of being utterly and completely lost trying to understand something, decided to call it quits, went to bed for the night, and woke up the next day with a total light-bulb moment. Suddenly it all made sense! That's because our brains need to process information, and they do that best when we're on a break. Helpful breaks include studying something completely different than what we were just stuck on, sleeping, exercising, hanging with friends, listening to music, or doing something creative. Helpful breaks do not include reading, scrolling, researching, or studying something like what we were stuck on.

Recognize when you're stuck, back up, and take a break. When you approach the information after doing these things, go at it a bit more slowly than before. Take your time with new concepts, and don't rush through them. And if you're still stuck after that, perhaps it's a concept you're not quite ready for and it's time to move on to the next section. You can always come back to it later to see if it makes more sense then.

Getting Started

Before we dive in, let's make sure you're set up for success. Do you have a journal ready to go? It doesn't need to be anything fancy; a simple notebook will do. However, if you'd like to make it special, go ahead and get creative. What's important is that you keep it and a pen with this book so you're ready when you need it. Anytime you're asked to reflect on a concept or to journal your answers to a question, grab them and start writing!

The next thing to consider is how you learn best. Most people tend to learn best in a quiet environment, but some find that having mellow music playing in the background helps. What tends to distract you from learning? If you're like most teens, you immediately thought of your phone, so put as many barriers between you and your phone as possible. Turn it off, put it in another room, or hand it over to a trusted person and tell them not to give it back for a specified amount of time. Make it hard on yourself to pick up and check your phone.

Also consider how you like to read and learn. Do you prefer being alone or around others? If you read or learn better with others, is there a friend who can read this book at the same time as you? Then you can discuss what you're learning and offer clarification to one another when needed. Is there a specific place you like to be when learning, such as your bedroom, the library, or the kitchen table? Keeping your learning environment fairly consistent helps prime your brain for learning. For example, if you usually go to your school library to study, your brain starts to associate the library with focus, attention, and learning. So as soon as you walk through the door, your brain is already getting ready to study without you even opening a book yet. If you don't yet have a designated place, use this book as your opportunity to find one. But just make sure you don't use the same place for different things, like using your bed for studying *and* sleeping. Your brain doesn't know what to do when you get into bed, so you'll end up having trouble studying and sleeping there.

One final thing to keep in mind is taking breaks when reading this book. Helping us when we feel stuck is not the only purpose for breaks. They also help us approach new material with fresh eyes. While reading this book, you don't have to end a chapter to take a break and instead can use new sections as a chance to stop. There are exercise sections in each chapter, and if you're able to, consider breaking after each one. This way you'll have time to do the exercise before jumping back into the book the next day. You may also want to take a smaller break if you notice that you're reading the same sentence over and over, feeling stuck on a concept or tool, or feeling like your body just can't sit still for another moment. If you're planning to come back to the book after a brief break, make sure you're doing something different from reading or learning while on the break. Go outside, move your body, talk to people, or play with your pet so your brain truly gets a break and a chance to reset.

Okay, I think you're ready to get started! Let's get going with some self-awareness. I'll meet you in chapter 1!

Foundational Skill: Self-Awareness

The first step in building overall emotional awareness is becoming more self-aware. Without this first foundational piece in place, everything else will crumble. Imagine how a person who isn't aware of their feelings, thoughts, or behaviors interacts with others, reacting to emotions and thoughts without knowing why, resulting in an inability to change their behaviors.

But what exactly does it mean to be self-aware? Self-awareness includes awareness of how we feel emotionally and physically, what we're thinking, and how we're behaving. When we're aware of our emotional and physical feelings, our thoughts, and our actions, we can choose to feel, think, and behave differently. But self-awareness also includes awareness of how others feel, being able to sense what they're thinking, and awareness of their actions. When we're aware of others' feelings, thoughts, and actions, we know when we need to make our own adjustments. We can't make those choices or adjustments without self-awareness.

Some teens are encouraged to be more self-aware than others. For instance, some families inspire self-awareness by checking in with one another about how they're feeling or what they're thinking. In these homes, teens don't get in trouble for experiencing negative feelings (although there might be consequences for what they did while experiencing them). Instead, family members can share their feelings and thoughts openly, without judgment or shame. Families that promote self-awareness also have members who are aware of what other family members are going through. Family members notice your actions and when your behavior is a bit out of the norm for you. You know that your family is more on this end of the spectrum if a parent or sibling gently points out a mood or behavior you're experiencing, asks you about your thoughts or feelings, or shares their own moods, emotions, thoughts, and actions with you.

In total contrast, some families discourage self-awareness in every way possible. In these households, teens aren't encouraged to talk about their feelings or thoughts. No one seems to notice what anyone else is feeling, and when people do share their feelings, they're met with ridicule, shame, judgment, or criticism. Family members don't seem to understand each other's behaviors and they misinterpret actions. You know your family leans to this end of the spectrum if feelings aren't shared by most, and when they are, people are mocked or told their feelings are wrong. You also might notice that people must guess what others are thinking since family members don't usually share their own thoughts. You might even observe how most family members are unaware of how their actions are connected to thoughts or feelings.

And then there are families that fall in between. Sometimes parents are great about shared feelings and other times, not so much. Sometimes siblings notice how you feel and if your behavior is different than usual, and other times, they don't. Self-awareness is a spectrum, and you might find that your family moves around on the spectrum from day to day, which is pretty normal. No family is perfect and you might even find that your family goes from one extreme to the other. That doesn't mean your family is awful or incapable of growing or changing. It just means that this is an area of weakness right now. They might be strong in other areas but just haven't really learned how to be more aware of their own feelings, thoughts, and behaviors or of the feelings, thoughts, and behaviors of others quite yet.

If you're in a family that discourages talking about feelings and thoughts, that isn't good at noticing how others are feeling, and where members respond negatively when feelings are shared, please know that it's still possible for *you* to build these skills. You don't need your whole family on board to become more self-aware. You may find that as you build your self-awareness, you even start to interact with family members in a more productive and healthy way. This may result in improved relationships, and you may start to feel better about yourself. And really, that's what this is all about. You're not trying to change anyone else here; you're focused on your own self-improvement.

So even if your family of origin doesn't value self-awareness, you can still develop this skill and use it to build the life you want. As you'll see, becoming more self-aware isn't something you turn on and off. As you learn and practice the skills in this chapter and the rest of the book, you'll start to notice new things about yourself that will become part of who you are. Perhaps you start identifying and labeling your emotions, which then leads to you calming yourself down the moment you realize you're getting upset (self-regulation). You may start to notice how you no longer go off on your friends, resulting in better friendships (interpersonal skills). And this new way of handling your emotions becomes natural, so you stop noticing it when you're doing it. You have become a person who calmly responds, even when experiencing a distressing emotion like hurt, jealousy, or embarrassment. Being self-aware is now just a natural part of your personality.

Self-Awareness vs. Self-Absorption

Before we dive deeper into self-awareness, let's make a distinction between self-awareness and self-absorption. Self-awareness is being aware of your own needs *and* others', which means that sometimes you'll put the needs of others above your own. Self-absorption is considering only your own needs, which means that you always put your own feelings and needs above others'. Consider Ally and see if you think she's being self-aware or self-absorbed.

Ally sits down for lunch at her regular table in the cafeteria. Her friend group is unusually quiet, and everyone is focused on Cam, who's staring at the table with his untouched food in front of him. No one says anything to Ally, so she starts talking about the Spanish test she's sure she just bombed and how unfairly the teacher grades everyone. No one acknowledges what she said, and she gets irritated: "Hey! Am I a ghost? Am I invisible?" Tess elbows her in the ribs and motions toward Cam with her eyes as she mouths, *His dad moved out last night.* Ally shrugs and starts pulling out her food from her lunch bag. "Cam…Cam…I know what you're feeling. I know what this is like for you. My uncle left his family too. I mean he was my uncle, not my dad, but we're a really close family, so he might as well have been my dad. When he left, it was so awful. Do you remember?" She looks around at everyone but no one's looking back. She continues, "I didn't come to school for a couple of days. I cried all the time. It was a really hard time. But I got through it. And you will too, Cam. If I got through it, you will too."

What do you think? Is she showing awareness of her needs and others' and recognizing that she should put Cam's needs in front of her own? Or is she considering only her own?

Ally is on the side of self-absorption rather than self-awareness. How do we know? Let's find the evidence: she didn't notice how her friend group was unusually quiet or focused on Cam; she didn't pay attention to the lack of response from others when she shared about her test; and when she learned about Cam's difficult experience, she made it about herself by equating his situation to something she'd once been through, which really wasn't like his at all. She lacked awareness of how others might be feeling and thinking, as well as awareness of how they were perceiving her. Her story reeks of self-absorption.

Self-awareness is both a gift and a responsibility. And it's okay if one falls short from time to time, but it's important to always do the best we can. You might find that sometimes you're like Ally, lost in your own thoughts, feelings, and problems while ignoring what's going on with friends right next to you. At other times, you might find that your self-awareness leads to a better understanding of what others are experiencing, resulting in closer relationships. Think of self-awareness as a seesaw that you're constantly trying to balance. One side is awareness of your own thoughts, feelings, and actions, and the other side is awareness of others' thoughts, feelings, and actions. While it's normal for a seesaw to become unbalanced from time to time, we don't want it to constantly be weighed down more on one side than the other.

What does it mean to be self-aware? Using Ally's situation, let's look at how different her interactions might have been if she'd been self-aware rather than self-absorbed.

Ally sits down for lunch at her regular table in the cafeteria. Her friend group is unusually quiet, and everyone is focused on Cam, who's staring at the table with his untouched food in front of him. No one says anything to Ally, and she's aware that the mood of the table is somber. She quietly asks the group, "Is everything okay?" Tess motions toward Cam and mouths, *His dad moved out last night.* Ally says, "I'm so sorry, Cam. Is there anything we can do to help right now?" Cam looks at her with sad eyes and shakes his head. Ally motions that they should all eat some lunch since everyone has food in front of them and starts pulling her own sandwich out of her lunch bag. She tells Cam, "I can't even imagine how you must be feeling right now. But just know that we're all here for you when you're ready to talk." She looks around at the group and asks if anyone has a funny story to share to help distract Cam for a bit so he can eat his lunch. Tess chimes in, "Ooooooh, I've got a good one...Cam, are you ready to hear about a certain science teacher with a fake British accent who accidently started speaking without it today?" Cam smiles and nods while opening his water bottle.

Ally's awareness of others' emotions, thoughts, and behaviors gave her the ability to be a good friend. She considered the mood of the table (awareness of others' emotions), realized that people were quiet (awareness of others' behaviors) and had food out in front of them (awareness of how others feel physically). She also showed a good understanding of what Cam could tolerate by asking for someone to share a funny story (awareness of how others perceive us).

Here are the components of self-awareness:

- Awareness of your own emotions—being able to identify and label your own feelings

- Awareness of your own physical sensations—understanding what different sensations mean and knowing when and how to connect physical sensations with emotions, thoughts, and actions

- Awareness of your own thoughts—knowing what thoughts are circulating inside your head and which ones actually deserve your attention

- Awareness of your own actions and behaviors—understanding your patterns of behavior and why you behave the way you do, knowing when your actions impact those around you

- Awareness of how others feel emotionally—being able to accurately assess how someone else is feeling based on their words, body language, what you know about them, and how they're currently behaving

- Awareness of how others feel physically—understanding how someone might be feeling physically in that moment based on their body language and words

- Awareness of how others think—being able to intuit or understand what someone else is thinking based on their body language, actions, feelings, and what you know about them

- Awareness of how others act and behave—being able to predict or understand someone else's behavior based on their feelings, body language, and what you know about them

- Awareness of how others perceive us—being able to read social cues or understand social context (for example, the ability to read the room).

Whew! That's a lot of awareness. But don't worry: we'll break it down and take it step by step.

Reflecting on Your Self-Awareness

How do you think you are in the different areas of self-awareness? Grab your journal and let's do some reflection. We'll use a scale of 1–10, where 1 means barely, 5 means kind of, and 10 means all the time.

How would you rate yourself on being able to identify and label your own emotions?

1	5	10
I barely notice what I'm feeling.	I notice the really intense emotions but not much else.	I pretty much know what I'm feeling at any given time of day.

How do you rate yourself on being able to accurately figure out how others are feeling?

1	5	10
I generally have little idea what those around me are feeling.	I notice when they're experiencing really strong feelings or doing things associated with really strong feelings like crying, storming out of a room, or laughing.	I'm focused on how those around me feel all the time.

Now that you've rated your awareness of emotions, I'd like you to take a moment to reflect. Use your journal to respond to these questions:

- How would a close friend or family member rate you?

- What would your best friend or your parent say about your awareness of your own feelings? Would they say that you generally communicate what you're feeling or that you shut down when upset?

- What would your best friend or your parent say about your awareness of how they feel? Would they say that you're great at noticing their feelings, or would they say that you barely consider their feelings at all?

- Do you pay too much attention to what others are feeling, to the point of ignoring your own feelings?

- Where do you see room for growth or change?

Next, we'll look at your awareness of your thoughts. Using your journal and the same 1–10 scale from above, where 1 means barely, 5 means kind of, and 10 means all the time:

How would you rate yourself on being able to identify and label your own thoughts?

1	5	10
I barely notice what I'm thinking.	I notice the really intense thoughts but not much else.	I pretty much know what I'm thinking at any given time of day.

How do you rate yourself on being able to accurately figure out what others are thinking?

1	5	10
I generally have little idea what those around me are thinking.	I notice when they share their thoughts or do things that show what they're thinking, like rushing around when they think they're going to be late or repeatedly texting someone because they think the person is mad at them.	I'm focused on how those around me think all the time.

Once again, I'd like you to take a moment to reflect. Use your journal to respond to these questions:

- How would a close friend or family member rate you?

- What would your best friend or your parent say about your awareness of your own thoughts? Would they say that you share your thoughts frequently or that you often say, "I don't know" when they ask what you're thinking?

- What would your best friend or your parent say about your awareness of what they think? Would they say you're great at noticing their thoughts or would they say that you rarely consider what they're thinking?

- Do you pay too much attention to what others are thinking, to the point of ignoring your own thoughts?

- Where do you see room for growth or change?

Brain Dumps

Time to become more aware of those feelings and thoughts. But before you do, you may be interested to know that a team of psychology experts from Queen's University in Canada found that the average person thinks over six thousand thoughts in a day (Tseng and Poppenk 2020). That's a lot of thinking! If we paid attention to every thought or treated every thought equally, we'd be exhausted. But that's what a lot of us do—we think that because we think it, it must be true. However, thoughts aren't facts (neither are feelings). To avoid mental exhaustion, we must learn to observe thoughts without giving attention to the unhelpful ones. To do this, you're going to do a *brain dump*.

A brain dump is when you allow every thought out of your head and every feeling out of your body and onto your paper. You write and write and write, without worrying about punctuation, spelling, grammar, or capitalization. The idea is to dump out every thought and feeling.

Before you start, the choice of time and place needs to be considered. Think of a time when you can do a brain dump later today or tomorrow. Pick a time when you won't be interrupted. I don't recommend doing this right before bed because we sometimes have a hard time shutting off our thoughts and feelings after this exercise is over, which can make sleeping very difficult.

Choose a time when you have something to do after the exercise (like eating dinner, hanging with friends, or walking the dog) so that your brain has something else to focus on. Schedule the time in your planner, set a reminder on your phone, or write it on a sticky note and put it somewhere you'll see it. Once you have scheduled your time, choose a place where you have some privacy and where you're not worried about someone reading over your shoulder.

When you're ready, set your timer for ten minutes. During the ten minutes, dump all your thoughts and feelings into your journal and keep going until the timer goes off. No cheating and stopping early either. You must write the entire time without checking social media or texts or anything else on your phone. Just write whatever comes to mind, no matter how silly or dumb it sounds to you.

Doing regular brain dumps will increase your awareness of thoughts and teach you how to notice the helpful ones while letting go of the unhelpful ones. They are great to do when you feel confused, anxious, content, excited, discouraged, hurt, distant, or proud. They're also great to do at the end of a long day to help clear your head a bit before winding down for the night. I recommend doing a brain dump daily.

Self-Awareness Meets Self-Regulation

There must be a balance between self-awareness and self-regulation. Researchers have found that if you're overly focused on how you feel, think, and act but lack the ability to regulate, you're not really helping yourself. In fact, you're likely making yourself feel worse. These researchers found that you're stuck in a negative emotional state, replaying a situation in your head, and unable to move on to something more productive or helpful. When people understand their emotions, thoughts, and behaviors, they're able to repair negative mood states. When they repair negative mood states, they cope better with stressful events and can minimize negative thoughts (Armstrong, Galligan, and Critchley 2011).

Self-awareness and self-regulation go together. And because self-regulation is such an important part of emotional intelligence, I'm including *lots* of ways to become more regulated. We'll start here and will build on this important skill in other areas.

Self-regulation is the ability to manage your emotions and keep your behavior in check. Knowing how to self-regulate decreases depression and anxiety while increasing self-esteem (Fernández-Berrocal et al. 2006). For instance, when you can improve your mood in challenging circumstances, you're less likely to make the situation worse, which will make you feel better about yourself.

Pretend that you've been working on building self-awareness and notice that you're feeling high anxiety in class because it's discussion day. You know you're going to have to participate in order to earn points, and self-awareness work has taught you that you get anxious talking in front of others. But now that you know this about yourself, you're able to intervene and change the intensity of the anxiety. If you can self-regulate by doing paced breathing, practicing mindfulness, and changing your self-talk (all tools you'll learn in this book!), you'll feel less anxious and be more likely to offer a valuable insight during discussion. On the flip side, if you can't self-regulate, you might start sweating, feel hot and flushed, and think that everyone is staring at you and noticing how anxious you are. You might even tell the teacher you're sick and leave to use the bathroom for the remainder of the class, missing out on your participation points.

Self-regulation is also a protective barrier against negative life events like fights with friends, break-ups, family conflict, or losing a loved one. Research shows that if you're proficient at self-regulation, you're even able to do it during emotionally intense situations (Armstrong, Galligan, and Critchley 2011). Think about it: if you know how to calm yourself down easily and practice it daily, you'll have the skill set in place for extremely hard circumstances. Suppose that you've been practicing the self-regulation tools in this book on a regular basis and have become pretty good at regulating yourself. You no longer blow up when upset and, instead, use a tool and can manage the situation well. And then your love breaks up with you completely out of the blue. You're floored, shocked, and overcome with intense sadness and anger. But then without even having to consciously think about it, you say that you need to take a break from the conversation and that you'll be back in fifteen minutes. Now that you're alone, you're able to use the intense exercise and paced breathing tools that you'll learn later in this book. You're still upset but you're not as dysregulated (moody or feeling out of control) as you were initially. You're able to resume the conversation without saying something cruel or hurtful.

Pay Attention

To be able to self-regulate, you must first know that you're dysregulated, which means you need to be aware of your emotions. This can be a really hard thing for many teens. You're just starting to build self-awareness, and in the next chapter, we'll dive into self-awareness of emotions. I realize you might not always know how you're feeling. Be patient with yourself. Practice paying attention to what you're feeling for now. Pay attention to the big feelings when they arise so that you start to notice when you're becoming dysregulated. The better you get at noticing the big feelings, the easier it'll be to recognize the smaller feelings.

You'll get access to a feeling wheel in the next chapter to help build your emotional vocabulary, so don't stress if you find you can identify your emotions only in simplistic terms like sad, mad, happy, or worried. Start where you are! Notice whatever feelings you can, whenever you can. All I'm asking for now is that you pay attention to your emotions. Observe them as they arise or once a feeling has already taken hold. And if this is difficult for you, that's totally fine. All that means is that you haven't learned this skill yet. It's a good thing you're reading this book.

Tools for Self-Regulation

Let's first cover three incredible self-regulation tools that you can begin using today. These three go together and are great for when you're feeling angry, hostile, frustrated, disappointed, helpless, embarrassed, or anxious. They can also be practiced independently of one another to manage feelings of sadness, jealousy, irritation, guilt, shame, loneliness, or insecurity.

Feeling labeling: Sometimes just identifying our emotions helps us feel better. It's as if labeling them takes away their power. It makes us feel more in control. Like I mentioned above, you might not always know how you're feeling and that's totally fine. You're going to learn more about emotions and build your emotional vocabulary in the next chapter. But for now, just start paying attention to how you're feeling by doing check-ins during the day—ask yourself, *What emotion am I feeling right now?* You're not judging the feeling or even questioning why you're feeling that way, you're simply labeling the feeling. When you notice that you're dysregulated (feeling moody or out of control), try and label as many of the feelings you're experiencing as you can. Pause and use the feeling wheel from the next chapter. Write them down if you need to. Labeling feelings is a great way to help regain some control and creates a pause so we're less likely to overreact or do something we'll regret later.

Taking a break: This favorite go-to tool is used by many and probably already one you do from time to time. Taking a break from an emotionally charged situation is a great way to regulate, but there's a caveat: you must come back to the situation. Taking a break doesn't mean walking away from an intense argument and then acting like it never happened. It means leaving to calm yourself down a few levels so that you can continue the discussion without yelling, hitting, hurting, or elevating. You might even need to let someone know what you're doing so they don't think you're leaving the discussion or avoiding the consequence. Breaks include going to your bedroom, taking a walk, going to the bathroom, getting a drink of water, or listening to music. And it's a break because while you're doing it, you're not thinking about the thing that upset you to begin with—you're fully engaging in whatever you're doing on the break. Which leads us to the third tool...

Mindfulness: If you've heard about mindfulness before, read this section anyway! There's a lot of misinformation out there on what mindfulness means, and many people think of an old man on a hill meditating while butterflies circle the bun on his head. That's not what mindfulness is. Mindfulness is when we fully engage with the present moment. That's it. It's that simple. We use as many of our senses as we can to allow our brains to participate in what's happening as we're doing it.

For example, if I'm being mindful while I go for a walk, I'm going to pay attention to the things I see and the sounds of my breath or passing traffic or the trees blowing in the wind. I'm also going to notice any smell like coffee from the café I walk by or flowers growing on a blossoming tree. I'll notice how my body feels with each step and see if I can feel the ground under my shoes and how the temperature of the air feels on my skin.

We can practice mindfulness anytime, anywhere, and with anyone, no matter what we're doing. We can be mindful while we eat, talk, or sit on a train or bus. We can be mindful alone or with others. We can practice when excited or exhausted. Mindfulness is a great way to self-regulate as it allows us to focus on the present moment rather than our emotions and thoughts.

Just like how you'll need to practice labeling feelings, you'll also need to practice mindfulness. But the more you practice and do it when it's easy (when you're regulated), the better you'll be at doing it when you really need it (when you're dysregulated). Here's a short reflection to get you started:

Imagine that you're hanging out with a friend at her house, watching movies, talking, and making bracelets for the school fundraiser later this week. She nonchalantly announces that Jake (the boy you've had a crush on *forever*) invited her to a bonfire next Saturday at his house, and she asks if you'd mind if she went since she knows about the crush. You're immediately aware of your physical sensations and notice that you feel hot and have a huge lump in your throat. You're aware of your feelings of hurt, jealousy, and embarrassment. You notice your thoughts: *How could she do this to me?* and *It's not fair. I've liked him forever!*

You decide that you need to take a break to calm down, and you say, "I'm feeling lots of things right now, and I don't want to say something I'll regret. I need ten minutes to calm down. We can talk about this when I get back." You go outside and practice mindfulness by noticing the cool temperature of the air on your skin, you smell the flowers blooming on a nearby tree, you walk around and pay attention to how your feet feel as they press into the ground with each step, you hear birds singing and cars passing by, and you start naming everything you can see. You don't pull out your phone to look at Jake's social media, you don't think about your friend and him as a couple, you don't ask yourself how a friend could do such a thing. You're focused on fully engaging in the present moment so you can self-regulate.

Self-regulation isn't about making hard or intense feelings disappear. Self-regulation decreases the intensity of such feelings so that we can respond in a way that's more helpful and productive.

Perhaps after regulating yourself, you decide that it's not that big a deal if your friend hangs out with Jake since you prefer to admire him from afar anyway. Or maybe you decide to tell her how you feel and talk it out together. Or you realize that you've never acted on this crush and it's not fair to make Jake off-limits to your friends while you do nothing about it. No matter the resolution, your self-regulation tools allowed you to respond from a place of calm (or at least less intense feelings) rather than react from the initial intense emotions, which would have made the situation considerably harder to manage.

Label, Take a Break, Be Mindful

Feeling labeling, taking a break, and mindfulness are three of my most used tools (by me and my clients!). The next time you experience an intense emotion—whether it's anger, anxiety, sadness, or frustration, I want you to label your feelings and take a break. But remember, you're not leaving the situation to never return! If there's another person involved, you're letting them know that you're taking a break to calm down and that you'll return in five to fifteen minutes. While you're on your break, practice mindfulness. Use as many of your five senses as possible to fully engage in the present moment. Name things you can see and hear. Touch what's around you and pay attention to how it feels. Smell the air and name the different odors your nose picks up. If there's anything you can taste, whether gum, candy, or a bit of clean snow from the ground, swirl it around in your mouth. Notice how using these tools changes the way you respond. You got this!

We're going to focus on emotional awareness next. So take a break, practice using your tools, do a brain dump or two, and I'll see you when you're ready to start learning about your emotions.

CHAPTER 2

Foundational Skill:
Self-Awareness of Emotions

Now that you have a better understanding of self-awareness in general, we're going to dive into awareness of your own emotions. Many people your age don't have a robust understanding of feelings and rely on basic feeling words like "sad," "mad," "happy," or "scared" to describe the emotional state of themselves and others. Perhaps you've seen this in yourself when you're struggling to explain how you feel. Or maybe you've noticed that others are better at pointing out what you're feeling than you are at figuring out your own emotions. There are many reasons why this happens, like not having the emotional vocabulary you need to describe your feelings; living in a family where emotions are ignored, denied, or not discussed frequently; or being afraid that awareness of your emotions will make them even stronger.

If you're someone who struggles to describe what you're feeling or you find that all your emotions are tangled into one knotty mess, you're going to love the feeling wheel. It will help you untangle the mess so you can better articulate what you're feeling. You'll expand your emotional vocabulary, and when you practice the emotional check-ins later in this chapter, you'll get better and better at describing your feelings. Building emotional awareness is a process and can take time. Be patient with yourself on this journey. You likely felt lost in your first month (or two) of your foreign language class, but with time, you probably started to understand your teacher better as they spoke to you in this new language. That will happen here too.

Or perhaps you're someone who lives in a family where emotions are ignored, denied, or not discussed frequently, so you've never really had the opportunity to recognize your feelings or the feelings of those around you. You're breaking the cycle! You're doing things differently than your family and, while that's a tough thing to do, you'll find that it's better for your own mental well-being. While your family may not usually identify the emotions of you or others, you still can. You can share your emotions with those you trust and will feel better since you're no longer holding them inside.

And if you're someone who's afraid that emotional awareness will unlock something inside you, making your feelings stronger and more difficult to control, please know that this is a normal fear. This is a huge reason why many people suppress their feelings and shove them deep down inside. They're afraid they'll lose control and end up in a rage or crying all the time. But in fact, when we acknowledge our feelings, the opposite ends up happening. Our feelings become less intense and have less power over us. When we allow ourselves to feel an emotion, when we label it for what it is (like depression, disappointment, or embarrassment), we're now in control. Because we *know* what we're feeling and we can choose to do something about it. But if you're still not convinced, please know that this book will give you the skills needed to handle difficult emotions in a healthy way.

In contrast, when we suppress a feeling and push it down inside, acting like it doesn't exist, the emotion is actually controlling us. We snap at others for seemingly no reason, or we appear tense or irritable to others, causing them to stay away. We then feel even worse because friends aren't calling or texting or because family members are frustrated with us. And because we keep suppressing our emotions, we think there's nothing we can do to feel better, so we blame everyone and everything around us. We say we snapped because Mom was nagging or we're irritable because the teacher was unfair. Friends aren't calling or texting because they care only about themselves, and family members are frustrated because they're mean. We think we're in control but really, we're in a free fall.

No matter your personal reason, you can improve your emotional awareness. You can build your emotional awareness and improve from any level. It doesn't matter if you walk through your day unaware of your feelings or if you notice only the extremes; we're going to build your emotional vocabulary so that you can better identify and label your feelings, whether they're small, large, or somewhere in between. In this chapter, we're also going to identify your triggers so that you have a better understanding of what sets you off or intensifies your emotions, which will help with overall emotional awareness. We'll also work on connecting emotions and actions to help you further expand your awareness. And finally, you'll learn how to tolerate discomfort and will get a chance to practice some new self-regulation tools that are based in self-soothing techniques.

Your Emotional Vocabulary

Just like we learn vocabulary words in biology or music, we also have vocabulary words for describing how we feel. You may even be familiar with feeling wheels; perhaps you've had teachers who hung them in classrooms or parents who encouraged you to use one. Feeling wheels are helpful tools in building our emotional vocabulary as well as in helping us identify and label our emotions. Remember that emotional awareness is an essential ingredient in emotional intelligence. And we can't self-regulate if we don't know what we're feeling.

Dr. Gloria Willcox created a helpful feeling wheel that we'll use here too (1982). You can find it at the back of the book or download the wheel at http://www.newharbinger.com/52083. I encourage you to make multiple copies of the wheel and hang one in your room, put one inside your planner, and tape one to the fridge. If you prefer a colorful version, I encourage you to color in your wheel with markers, crayons, or colored pencils (coloring is good for our mental wellness!). Take a picture of it, and store it on your phone or make it a screen saver. Create easy access to the feeling wheel so you can look at it no matter where you are. As you start to better understand your emotions, please notice that I'm using the words "feelings" and "emotions" interchangeably. If you ever choose to dive deep, deep, deep into psychology, you'll learn differences between the two words; however, for most people, feelings and emotions will be synonymous.

You'll notice how the inner circle of the wheel includes basic feelings of sad, mad, scared, joyful, powerful, and peaceful. The middle and outer circles demonstrate more specific emotions related to each basic one. While you're building your emotional vocabulary, start with identifying your basic feeling first. Then look to the middle and outer circles to get more specific. For example, someone might say they're feeling mad initially but upon further reflection, they're able to identify that they're actually feeling hurt and jealous. Mad is a more general description of an emotion, while hurt and jealous give us a clearer picture of what their internal experience is really like.

Start using the wheel when you're unsure of how you're feeling, and find a basic emotion that most closely matches your feeling. It doesn't need to be an exact match, just close enough. Then stay within the same triangle or color of your identified basic feeling and look at the middle and outer circles and find the closest match to what you're feeling. You can also use the wheel when you know how you're feeling to see if there's a better feeling word on there to describe your current emotional state.

Dr. Willcox notes that not all emotions are shown on this feeling wheel, but I think it's a pretty good start. She also reminds people that you can feel more than one of the emotions on the wheel at the same time. I know I have. If you're having trouble finding your feeling on the wheel, it could be that it's not on there or that you're feeling several at the same time. But again, try and find the closest match, even if it doesn't perfectly describe the emotion you're currently experiencing. You can also pick multiple emotions and see if choosing several helps describe your current state.

Some people have difficulty figuring out their emotion in the moment, and if that's like you, practice pausing whenever you notice a change in feeling. Look at the feeling wheel and locate the closest match to the feeling you just had, and then see if you can find your current emotion. Practice pausing no matter how small the change in emotion and whether it's a negative or positive change. You're pausing to build your emotional vocabulary, so the more you do it, the easier it'll get to label your feelings.

Look at the feeling wheel now. Close your eyes and put your finger anywhere on the wheel. When you open your eyes and see which feeling you landed on, think of a time when you felt that emotion. Grab your journal and answer these questions:

- Who were you with?

- What were you doing?

- Were there any physical signs that alerted you to the feeling, such as trembling telling you it was anxiety or a pit in your stomach telling you it was ashamed?

- Did you know the emotion you were experiencing at the time, or was it in hindsight that you figured it out?

Examine the feeling wheel again and this time, consider which feelings you find yourself noticing the most and which ones you barely experience. In your journal, reflect on these questions:

- Which emotions are you most aware of?

- Which emotions do you think you barely experience at all?

- Do you tend to notice more basic feelings of the inner wheel most of the time, or do you also notice the specific ones on the middle and outer circles?

- · Do you notice any patterns? (Perhaps you're hyperaware of negative emotions but barely notice positive ones. Or maybe you're more likely to notice the basic feelings but rarely observe more specific ones.) Why do you think that is?

Tolerating Discomfort

While it's not included on the feeling wheel, discomfort is an emotional response to many situations like hard conversations with loved ones, uncertainty about the future, or making tough decisions. But discomfort is also a common physical response to a variety of emotions such as boredom, insecurity, anxiety, or loneliness. (If it were up to me, I'd add discomfort to the middle circle of the scared piece of the pie.) Basically, discomfort can show up as an emotion and as a physical feeling. Many teens and young adults don't know how to tolerate discomfort and end up doing things to avoid it, like going on their phones, drinking, smoking, picking at their bodies, or pacing. But whether emotional or behavioral, discomfort is a normal part of life, and if you want to learn how to manage your feelings better, you're also going to have to learn how to tolerate discomfort.

Do you notice when you experience discomfort? If you answered no, it's likely because you're not giving yourself a chance to even feel it. You're probably jumping on your phone or engaging in another avoidance tactic the second discomfort starts to make an appearance. You're going to have to start paying attention to why you're picking up your phone, drinking, smoking, picking, or pacing. You'll have to pause the moment you do one of those things and ask yourself, *What's making me uncomfortable right now?* On the flip side, if you answered yes to noticing discomfort, what are some things that incite discomfort in you? When do you notice it? How are you currently managing it?

To learn how to tolerate discomfort, you'll need to acknowledge it, understand why you're feeling it, and sit with it. We don't avoid the feeling. Instead, we acknowledge it (*I'm feeling discomfort right now*). We understand the reason (*This conversation is really hard but necessary*). And we stay put (*I can continue this conversation despite my discomfort*). We don't get on our phones, leave, or distract from the discomfort. We acknowledge the feeling, understand why, and stay in the situation (if it's a safe one). Tolerating discomfort is *hard*. No one likes it. But we can't run from it forever.

I once had a client who felt discomfort whenever she was lonely. To deal with these feelings, she'd pick up her phone, get on social media, and scroll. She'd see friends hanging out without her and people engaging in fun things, which would then make her feel even lonelier. Since she was lonelier, her discomfort intensified and scrolling wasn't enough to avoid the feeling, so she'd pick at scabs, cuticles, bug bites, pimples, or whatever other imperfections she could find on her body. She'd notice the damage of her picking and feel out of control. She didn't know what to do.

What do you think we did in our work together? We worked on learning how to tolerate discomfort. She needed to learn how to tolerate the discomfort of being lonely. She learned how to acknowledge her emotions first (*I'm feeling lonely, which is really uncomfortable*). She worked to understand why (*I don't have anyone to hang out with today*). And she learned how to stay in her emotions (*These feelings are normal, they won't kill me. I can feel lonely and uncomfortable as I move through my day*). She didn't avoid or distract herself from her feelings, and instead allowed herself to feel the emotions while she did the things she needed to do that day, like showering, cleaning her room, and doing laundry. Eventually the loneliness and discomfort decreased enough that she was able focus on things she enjoyed and wanted to do.

Take a moment right now to consider how you're feeling emotionally. Grab your journal and feeling wheel and set a timer for five minutes. Write about how you feel right now and how you felt earlier today. Don't judge or critique the feelings. Notice and observe them. Answer these questions:

- How are you feeling right now? Using the feeling wheel, are you bored, tired, confused, or discouraged? Or are you feeling thoughtful, serene, pensive, or content? Perhaps you're anxious and overwhelmed? Or excited and confident?

- Think of your emotions as visitors you're describing. How do they behave? How long have they been hanging around? How have they been affecting you?

- How would you describe any emotions you've experienced today?

- What was your general mood for the day?

Now that you're done with your five minutes of journaling, let's reflect on how the experience was for you.

- How did it feel to identify your emotions? What was the experience like for you?

- What did you notice about identifying the best-fitting emotion(s)?

- Which feelings did you keep coming back to? Which ones did you notice that you feel more than others?

Make any notes on your reflections in your journal before you move on.

If you found that your emotional vocabulary is limited, that's perfectly fine. This is a skill that can be built.

The Difference Between Emotion and Mood

Many people use the words "emotion" and "mood" interchangeably, but there's actually a difference. According to *Oxford Dictionaries Online*, an emotion is a state of mind based on your circumstances, mood, or relationships. Notice how the word "mood" is included in this definition? Emotions can be dependent on your mood. The same dictionary defines a mood as a temporary state of mind. Does that clear things up for you? Probably not—and now you can see why people use them interchangeably!

The best way to think of the difference between emotions and moods is that moods last longer and are the container that holds your emotions. Using school as an analogy, it's like your mood is the school and your emotions are a class. Just like how you can be at school but sitting in geometry class, you can be in an irritable mood but still feel excited when you get asked out by your crush. Or your mood might be calm but then you feel anxious when you see your test score. Sometimes your emotion is strong enough to change your mood, and sometimes your mood is strong enough to dampen your emotion. For example, you keep feeling excitement (emotion) about the idea of going out with your crush, so your irritability (mood) changes to optimism. Or you're in such a state of calm (mood) that the anxiety (emotion) about the undesired test score barely registers on your emotional radar.

As you're becoming familiar with the feeling wheel and all the different words on it, start seeing if you can tell the difference between an emotion and a mood. When you identify your feeling, ask yourself how long you've had the emotion and if it's based on a situation, relationship, or general state of mind. If it's been coming and going or is based on circumstance or an interaction with someone else, or because of a general state of mind, congratulations! You've discovered an emotion. But if the feeling you've identified is more of a general state of mind that you've had for several hours and not due to a situation or relationship, congratulations! You've discovered a mood! Practice labeling it correctly by noting My *current emotion is* _____ or My *current mood is* _____ and choosing one or two of the feeling words from the wheel.

As you do this, you might notice that sometimes your mood and emotions are in complete harmony. For example, your mood is peaceful and your current emotion is content. Or your mood is hostile and your current emotion is irritated. Other times you'll notice that your mood and emotions contrast with each other and don't make much sense. Perhaps your mood is depressed but your current emotion is amused. Or maybe your mood is playful but your emotion is discouraged. It can be confusing when our moods and emotions are in conflict with one another, but this is perfectly normal. And this is also why it's beneficial to practice labeling your mood and emotion when you use the feeling wheel. You'll learn to recognize whether the identified feeling is based on a situation, mood, or relationship (emotion) or if it's a temporary state of mind (mood).

Identifying Patterns

Another aspect of emotional awareness is knowing your own patterns, especially when it comes to strong negative reactions. It's important to understand what might create a strong emotional reaction so you can see the storm coming and prepare accordingly. Let's say you know how awful you feel when friends get together without you. You know that you feel rejected and hostile whenever you see posts of them doing things you weren't invited to, or you feel lonely and angry when you hear friends talking about something they did together that you were unable to attend.

Because you've been working so hard on building your emotional awareness and know this pattern in yourself, you decide to not get on social media when you're home alone and bored, fearing that your friend group is doing something fun without you. Instead, you take your dog for a walk. At school, because you've been working on self-regulation skills, you pull out tools from chapter 1 the moment you overhear them talking about the fun they had at last night's basketball game, which you couldn't make because you had to drive your brother to hockey. You identify your feelings (lonely and angry), take a break by going to the water fountain, and practice mindfulness by focusing on how cold the water is, the sounds of others in the halls, and the way the sun is reflecting off the lockers.

Many teens and young adults don't know or understand their patterns, so they walk through life feeling as though their emotions are out of control. They experience strong negative emotional reactions to events but don't understand why. They feel confused and disoriented by their responses without recognizing that the same thing keeps happening over and over—they see friends hanging out together on social media, feel lonely, and then blow up at their mom for no reason. They experience the same strong reaction to the same types of events. Common events that create strong emotional reactions include being told no, receiving negative or critical feedback, fighting with friends or family members, receiving an undesired score or grade, thinking that people are laughing at them, feeling ignored or rejected, and feeling intentionally left out of a social situation or group. You might have other specific things that make you feel intensely anxious or overwhelmed, like current events, family problems, or physical health concerns.

Take a moment to notice patterns by responding to these questions in your journal:

- Consider the common and specific events listed in the previous paragraph. Which ones create strong negative reactions for you? List them in your journal.

- Think of the last time you felt out of control of your emotions or behaviors and describe the situation. Who was with you? What were you doing? What happened right before you experienced the strong reaction? What were you thinking?

- Look at the feeling wheel and list the emotions that are most difficult for you to manage. Which feelings do you struggle to control much of the time?

Connecting Emotions with Behaviors

Now that you've been thinking a bit about your own patterns, let's consider how your feelings are connected to your actions. When you're experiencing a strong negative emotion, how do you tend to behave? For example, some people slam doors or drawers when feeling angry while fighting with family members; others cry. Some people isolate and shut down when overwhelmed with responsibility, while others start arguments for no obvious reason. Consider your pattern list from the previous exercise and make notes about how you behave when you react strongly. How do you act when pushed to your emotional limits?

Now let's focus on feelings. Look at the feeling wheel again. Let's consider how you *emotionally* respond to situations. To illustrate, many people tend to feel isolated when they've been left out or rejected by friends. People also typically feel discouraged when watching undesired current events unfold. Which emotions on the feeling wheel do you experience when you're having a strong reaction? Consider your list of difficult-to-manage emotions from the last exercise. Are there any new ones to add to that list?

Strong reactions can also occur for other reasons, and we might notice patterns here as well. Sometimes we can predict how we'll feel, based on our behaviors. I know that if I didn't sleep well the night before, I'm much more likely to feel irritated by small things throughout the day. I also know that if I spend too much time mindlessly scrolling on my phone, I'm going to feel apathetic later. On the other hand, I know that I'm going to feel proud after a good workout or optimistic when I've spent time in nature.

Becoming familiar with how you respond emotionally to different situations will help you make better choices. If you know that having a disorganized desk makes you feel overwhelmed, you'll be more likely to keep it in shape. And if you know that you become easily frustrated when hungry, you'll be sure to keep snacks on hand no matter where you are. So as you pay attention to your patterns, also notice how different behaviors affect your emotional state.

We're going to have a little fun with this exercise.

- Grab whatever device you use to listen to music.

- Now pick one of your absolute favorite songs.

- Before you play it, make sure no one's about to disturb or disrupt you; then get into a comfortable position so you can fully absorb the song.

- Grab your journal and make a note of your overall mood and your current feeling(s). Use the feeling wheel if you need help identifying your mood and feeling(s).

You're going to listen to the song in just a moment, and make sure when you do, you really listen to the beat, the lyrics, the undertones…everything.

- Tune out everything else and tune into this song.

- Once you're done with the song, grab your journal make a note of your current mood and feeling(s).

- What changes occurred from listening to the song?

Did you find yourself jumping up and down, dancing, and ready to mosh, or did your song put you into a state of relaxation or calm? Music is just one of the many things that creates instant change in our emotions and behaviors, so start paying attention to what you're listening to and how it's affecting you.

Self-Soothing Strategies

By now, you've heard the term "self-regulation" enough to know what it means (our ability to manage emotions and behaviors) and how it's a huge part of emotional intelligence. I mean, what's the point of learning all this awareness stuff if we're not going to do anything with it, right? But what you might not know is that we sometimes need to be picky about how we self-regulate.

Depending on our emotions, moods, and circumstances, we might prefer one self-regulation tool over another. In fact, we might even find that certain self-regulation tools make things *worse*, not better. Do you remember the three tools you learned in the previous chapter (hint: feeling labeling, taking a break, and mindfulness)? I started with those three because they're generally helpful ones no matter what your emotions, mood, and circumstances are. But there are some that aren't.

In this section, we're going to focus on two tools that are good for when you need to soothe yourself. How do you know when you need self-soothing tools? When the emotion or mood you're experiencing can't be problem-solved and it isn't responding to words, logic, or reasoning (Pittman and Karle 2015). Emotions and moods that respond well to self-soothing tools include (but aren't limited to) hurt, critical, discouraged, embarrassed, inferior, and lonely. You might find that self-soothing tools work well for other emotions and moods too, so be sure to practice so you know what works best for you.

Imagine that you're feeling sad but don't really know why. When you try and figure out what's making you so sad, you can't come up with a single thing to actually be sad about. Yet you feel on the verge of tears, have a lump in your throat, and are low energy. Or maybe you're experiencing anxiety and feel jittery and tense. And when you think about it, you realize you're anxious about a hurricane in another state where your relatives had to evacuate. You feel helpless since there's nothing you can do to change the circumstances and don't know what to do to change your feelings.

This is when self-soothing tools come into play. When you think about self-soothing, I want you to imagine comforting a new dog that your family just adopted from the shelter. What would you do if your new dog were afraid of the vacuum, blender, or other loud things in your home? You wouldn't say, "Oh don't worry, sweet Derby. That's just Dad making smoothies in the kitchen. He'll be done soon." No! You know that you can't rationalize or talk with your dog to calm her down when she's anxious. Instead, you might sit next to little

Derby on the floor, slowly running your hand down her back and whispering comforting messages into her floppy ears until she stops shaking. Rhythmic movement, gentle sounds, and light touches are all self-soothing tools.

Tools for Self-Soothing

Here are two of my favorite self-soothing tools that you can begin using the next time you feel an unwanted emotion and can't explain why. These tools aren't meant to distract you; rather, they're here to regulate you. Because when we're dysregulated, we're more likely to make poor choices, engage in unhealthy behaviors like smoking or drinking, and respond to others in negative ways.

Rhythmic or gentle movement: Remember sweet Derby? She calmed down with gentle pats and a calming voice. You might prefer lightly brushing your hair or calming music. Rhythmic movements also include rocking in a rocking chair, swing, or hammock. Even playing with a yo-yo or bouncy ball works. If you don't have one of those available, try gently hugging yourself around your rib cage while swaying side to side. Anything that provides a slow, gentle, rhythmic movement will work.

Use rhythmic movements to calm down, pause, de-escalate, or comfort yourself. Rhythmic movements help to calm down the central nervous system when it's excited, whether in a good or bad way (Staras, Chang, and Gilbey 2001). And when our central nervous system is more regulated, we respond in healthier and more productive ways. Suppose that you're feeling insecure and have tried giving yourself a pep talk, which only made you feel worse. You decide to try a rhythmic movement and walk to the nearby park and hop on a swing. You start off slowly moving side to side, without even taking your feet off the ground. But as you do this, you notice that you're feeling different—a bit less insecure and a bit more peaceful. You pick up the pace and start swinging more, lifting your feet off the ground and pumping your legs. The back-and-forth movement helps, and soon you forget what brought you to the park to begin with. You walk home feeling refreshed and recharged.

Paced breathing: Whether we want it to our not, our breathing changes when we're stressed out. It becomes more rapid and shallower. But when we're self-aware, we notice these types of physiological changes that occur naturally, and we choose to change them. Dr. Andrew Weil, a practitioner of natural and preventive medicine, developed my favorite breathing technique, which he calls the relaxing breath exercise. You can find it online at https://www.drweil .com/health-wellness/body-mind-spirit/stress-anxiety/breathing-three -exercises. It's easy, simple, and can be done anywhere. And most important, it works. Like any breathing technique, we want inhales to come in through the nose and exhales to go out through the mouth.

- Inhale through your nose for four seconds.

- Hold for seven seconds.

- Exhale through your mouth for eight seconds.

This completes one cycle. Do three to five cycles to regulate yourself.

Emotional Check-ins

You've really been learning and thinking about your emotions in this chapter, and we want to keep that ball rolling! To do that, you're going to start doing *emotional check-ins*. An emotional check-in is exactly what it sounds like— you're checking in on how you're feeling. You can check in on both your current emotional state and your mood. When you're first starting off, it's good practice to do an emotional check-in once an hour while you're awake. Later, you won't need to do it as often. You might want to set a reminder or alert to go off on your phone hourly so you remember to do this.

To do an emotional check-in, follow these steps:

- Look at your feeling wheel and see what your current emotion is. Write it down, along with the time and day, in your journal.

- Look at the feeling wheel again and identify your mood. Write it down, along with the time and day, in your journal.

- Are your current emotion and mood in alignment, where they're similar or complement one another? Or are they vastly different, where they seem to be opposite or in conflict with each other? Make any notes about this in your journal.

Over time, you might start to notice patterns between your emotions, mood, and schedule. As you get better at identifying your emotions and moods, you can start to decrease how often you do an emotional check-in. Perhaps you do it at each meal, so it becomes an easy habit to remember. Or maybe you journal each morning when you awake and again at bedtime, and you include emotional check-ins during that time. Either way, make sure you're taking time each day to notice your emotions.

CHAPTER 3

Foundational Skill: Self-Awareness of Thoughts

Good job! You're becoming an expert in recognizing, understanding, and changing your emotions. That means it's time to examine those thoughts. Like emotional awareness, where you learned how to notice and identify your emotions, thought awareness is when you notice and identify your thoughts. Self-awareness of thoughts means knowing what thoughts are circulating inside your head and which ones actually deserve your attention.

Notice how there are two parts: (1) awareness of your thoughts and (2) knowing which ones get attention and which ones should be ignored. Both parts can be difficult, but both are skills that can be developed. You might find that you're aware of your thoughts but that you tend to get hung up on thoughts that make you feel worse. Or you might find that you aren't aware of your thoughts in the moment but just know you feel upset; however, after some reflection and contemplation, you realize what you were thinking at the time you were upset. This chapter will help you no matter where you fall on the continuum.

When building your self-awareness of thoughts, it's important to practice both being aware of thoughts and understanding which get your attention. If you only practice awareness of your thoughts without knowing which ones get attention, you'll be lost in all your thoughts. (Remember the researchers from Queen's University in chapter 1 who identified that the average person thinks six thousand thoughts a day? We wouldn't have time for anything else if we paid attention to each one.) Plus, you'll likely end up giving attention to thoughts that don't really deserve it—the ones that aren't based in fact or that you wouldn't say to someone you care about. So this chapter isn't just about becoming aware of your thoughts, it's also about recognizing which ones are helpful and which ones are hurtful. And because we know that awareness without regulation leads to *rumination* (getting stuck on negative thoughts), we'll also be adding some thought-based self-regulation tools.

Thought awareness is one of the key elements of *cognitive behavioral therapy* (CBT), which is an effective, popular, and evidence-based form of therapy. CBT comes out of the foundational assumption that thoughts, emotions, and behaviors are all connected. As a psychologist who uses CBT in much of my work with clients, I focus immensely on the thoughts behind feelings and actions because I know that if we can change those thoughts, emotion and behavior change will follow.

Thought awareness, whether we're doing CBT or not, can give us a good understanding of the impact of our thoughts on our feelings and actions. Once we have this understanding, we'll know which thoughts we should keep and which to let go of. Let's break this down.

Michael is getting ready for tryouts for the high school baseball team. He played on the freshman team last year and is hoping to skip the junior varsity team and move straight to varsity this year. As he heads into the locker room, he remembers what his mom told him last night: *Just focus on playing and nothing else. Don't worry about how others are doing. Just worry about yourself.* But as soon as he rounds the corner and sees the other players, he thinks about how much better they all are than him and that he'll never make it to varsity this year. He notices butterflies in his stomach and feels queasy. Other players say hello and he barely acknowledges them. Instead, he thinks of how they're going to laugh at him when he doesn't make the team. When everyone else is joking around during warm-ups, he's off to the side by himself. The freshman coach from last year calls out to him, "Michael! Nice to see you back again this year!" Michael gives a halfhearted wave back and quickly shifts his gaze to the ground.

Grab your journal. I'm going to walk you through this exercise, using Michael as an example, while you fill in each area with your own information.

Think of a situation you experienced recently where you were not so happy about the way you handled it. Perhaps you didn't do what you wanted to do or behaved in a way you're not proud to admit. Briefly write about this situation in your journal, leaving out details, feelings, thoughts, judgment, and criticism. For Michael, his situation is baseball tryouts.

What thoughts did you have at the time of the situation? Try and put yourself back in the situation and identify what thoughts were going through your head at the time. You may need to really pause and think about this. It can be hard to recall your thoughts, especially if you're not used to doing it. Take your time and, if you need to, guess what you were thinking and write those thoughts down. Michael's thoughts were that the other players were better than him, that he'd never make varsity, and that others will laugh at him when he doesn't make the team.

What feelings did you experience during the situation? Put yourself back in it and try and really feel the emotions. You can list emotions and physical feelings. How did your thoughts impact your feelings? Michael's feelings were nervousness, butterflies in his stomach, and nausea.

How did you behave? What impact did your thoughts and feelings have on your actions? Use your observational skills to note how you were impacted; you're not judging or criticizing yourself here. You're just an observer looking back to learn. Did you avoid something because of your feelings or thoughts? Did you behave in an unkind way? What did you do that could be considered a direct result of your thoughts or feelings? Write about it in your journal. For Michael, his thoughts and feelings caused him to ignore the other players who said hello to him and keep to himself during warm-ups, and he gave a minimal response to last year's coach.

Let's rewrite Michael's story as though he's been working on his emotional intelligence. He's aware of his thoughts and the impact they have on his feelings. And he knows how to change his thoughts when necessary.

Michael is getting ready for tryouts for the high school baseball team. He played on the freshman team last year and is hoping to skip the junior varsity team and move straight to varsity this year. As he heads into the locker room, he remembers what his mom told him last night: *Just focus on playing and nothing else. Don't worry about how others are doing. Just worry about yourself.* He feels anxious and notices butterflies starting to circle in his stomach. He rounds the corner and, when he sees the other players, he decides to start thinking about what he knows to be true right now. He focuses his thinking on how much he's been practicing lately, how much he's grown as a player, and how all he can do is try his best. He reminds himself that he'll be okay no matter which team he ends up on. He feels less nervous and is ready to change with the rest of the players. He listens in when others joke around, laughs when they tease him, and even joins in a bit. When last year's coach calls out to him, he gives a big smile and waves back.

Grab your journal again. We're going to go through the same exercise as before but with a twist. Again, we'll use Michael as an example as you fill in each area with your own information.

Using the same situation from the previous exercise, briefly write it out in your journal again. For Michael, his situation is baseball tryouts.

This time let's change those thoughts. What thoughts would have helped you feel more confident? What thoughts would have made you more courageous, brave, calm, or content? You may need to really pause and think about this. It can be hard to change our thoughts, but really try to put yourself back in that situation and think of a best friend, parent, coach, or teacher if needed. What would they have said to you at the time to help you through it? Those comments might work as your new thoughts. Or you can consider what you know to be true for yourself like Michael did. Michael's thoughts were about how much he's been practicing lately, that he's grown as a player and just needs to try his best, and that he'll be okay no matter which team he ends up on.

How would your feelings have changed because of your new thoughts? You can list your new emotions and physical feelings. Michael felt less nervous and more ready.

How would you have behaved? What impact would your new thoughts and feelings have on your actions? Would you do something brave or courageous because of your new feelings or thoughts? Would you behave in an extra kind way? What would you do that could be considered a direct result of your thoughts or feelings? Write about it in your journal. For Michael, his new thoughts and feelings caused him to joke around with the other players and respond to his old coach in a friendly manner.

Look back at your feelings and behaviors from the first example and compare them to those from this example. How are your feelings different? How did your behavior change? Michael felt less nervous and acted more confident.

When we examine the two different exercises, it's easy to see the power of our thoughts. You see, it wasn't the situation in either example that caused Michael or you to feel or behave in a certain way. The situation was the same in both examples. It was the thoughts that did it. For Michael, when he compared himself with others and thought about not making the team, he felt anxious and withdrew from others and acted more insecure. But when he focused on what he knew to be true about his abilities, he was able to feel less nervous and to engage with others in a positive way. While these two examples might make a clean and easy case for the power of our thoughts, unfortunately, it's not always that easy to see in the moment. But don't sweat it, we're going to dive into this more next.

Identifying Thoughts

Michael likely had lots of other thoughts swirling around in his head besides the ones he noticed; however, the others probably had very little impact on how he felt or what he was doing. And that's usually how it goes: we have a whole lot of thoughts that have zero impact on how we feel or behave, so we don't really need to pay attention to those. For instance, Michael probably had thoughts about something he learned in a class, something he overheard someone say, weekend plans, and maybe even thoughts about what's going to happen next in a series he's watching. But since none of those things created strong emotions or made him behave differently, he likely barely even noticed them.

But then there are the thoughts that make us feel nervous, excited, judged, loved, disappointed, or optimistic. These are the thoughts that cause us to isolate, avoid, show affection, quit, keep going, shut down, or speak up. Thoughts that are impacting us, whether helpful or hurtful, are the ones we need to notice. These are the thoughts that are going to either push us forward or hold us back from being versions of ourselves that we can be proud of. Initially, we may have to work backward to find the thoughts creating the feelings and behaviors. This means paying attention to our feelings and actions and then figuring out what we were thinking to create those emotions and actions.

When you're first starting off building thought awareness, you'll want to question your feelings and behaviors to identify the underlying thoughts. Here are some thought categories you can use to help you identify what type of thought you had:

- **Motivational thoughts** push us to go outside our comfort zone and inspire us to do something challenging. They cheer us on, inspire us, and tell us we can accomplish our goals.

- **Instructional thoughts** might sound more like a coach, teacher, or parent. They give us direction and remind us of what we need to be doing in the moment. They could even be technical, step-by-step instructions on what to do.

- **Factual thoughts** include those we can back up with solid, objective evidence (basically, they'd hold up in a court of law). Thoughts about the date of your best friend's birthday, your dentist appointment, things you're learning in class, or that you're supposed to pick up your little sister after tennis.

- **Critical thoughts** include ruthless and condemning thoughts about others or about yourself. These thoughts are subjective and could be easily disputed by someone else.

- **Judgmental thoughts** include harsh self-assessments, kind of like an inner bully, and include judging others cruelly or severely.

- **Narrative thoughts** include that inner voice talking about what you're doing or telling you what to do next. Think of the narrator in a movie; we can have that same kind of voice in our heads.

- **Observational thoughts** are those where you're watching someone or something and noticing new information. Perhaps picking up on their accent, how they move their body, or a new haircut.

- **Random thoughts** typically have no impact on behaviors or feelings. These are the thoughts that swirl around in our heads without creating much change at all: thoughts about the series you're watching, things you overheard in the hall, or a dream you had earlier this week.

Changing Thoughts

Now that we've learned how to identify our thoughts, we need to figure out how to reframe problematic thoughts. Otherwise, we'll just get buried in the unhelpful thoughts, unable to do the things we really want to do. Reframing a thought is just a fancy way of saying thinking of something differently. It sounds simple but can be quite difficult. Just think of a time you were absolutely 100 percent sure of something—maybe that a friend was mad at you, you bombed a test, or you were going to get fired—and someone in your life tried to get you to see an alternative. Perhaps they pointed out another way of considering your friend's behavior, that you've never failed a test in that particular class before, or that the mistake at work really wasn't as bad as you thought. But you were so sure of your thoughts that you couldn't be convinced otherwise. That is, until you saw your friend the next day and they were back to normal, you got your test back and realized you didn't even come close to bombing, or your manager asked you to work more hours during your shift the following day. You suddenly realized how silly and wrong you had been!

The point of reframing is to understand the alternative way of thinking about the situation *before* you actually get any sort of resolution. Reframing prevents our brains from going absolutely haywire and taking us into a dark place where no one likes us, we're never going to graduate, or no one will ever hire us again. It gives us the opportunity to consider other options and provides us with a different perspective on the situation.

Reframing can occur with the help of others or by yourself. You might notice that a friend, partner, or family member is really good at helping you reframe. Or perhaps you have a coach, therapist, or teacher who gently points out new ways to think of hard situations. These folks are keepers. People who can help you reframe are good people to have in your corner. Take a moment to think of who helps you reframe your unhelpful thoughts, and make a list in your journal. These are individuals you'll want to go to first when you feel overwhelmed with negative thinking. They are your guides to getting out of negative thinking and rumination.

We can't always count on others to help with reframing thoughts. Sometimes they're unavailable, sometimes we need to be able to reframe quickly on the spot; most of the time we need to be able to do this on our own. Ultimately, you'll want to be able to reframe internally, but when you're learning how to do it at the beginning, practice externally and write it out. You'll do this on your own in just a moment, but here's an example. Suppose that you're completely positive your friend is mad at you because they barely spoke to you at lunch and you catch yourself in need of a reframe. You grab a sheet of paper and brainstorm alternative ways of thinking about the situation. You think of what the best-case scenario is, what the worst-case scenario is, and how others might view the situation. You might write down (1) they're having a hard day; (2) they were in a quiet mood; (3) they have new friends they enjoy talking to at lunch; (4) they had a lot on their mind; (5) they've decided they no longer want to be friends with you. Next you consider the options you wrote down and choose the one that seems most likely. Perhaps you decide to choose the first option since you really have no other evidence that your friend is mad at you, and since you've been friends for a long time, you know they're not one to drop you just because they have new friends. You also consider the facts that they're taking really hard classes right now and it's midsemester, which tends to be more intense. You circle option one, cross out all the others, and repeat it over and over to yourself. Now you can assume that option one is true and go about your day. You just reframed your thought!

Practice doing this externally by thinking of a situation where you felt confused, frustrated, or upset. Perhaps someone said something that rubbed you the wrong way or something didn't turn out the way you wanted it to. Try and think of something that happened in the last two weeks. Grab your journal and write about it.

Brainstorm three to five alternative ways of thinking about the situation. Here are some prompts to get you started:

- What are some possible things going on with the other person?

- How might the situation look to a neutral observer?

- What can you learn from the situation?

- What capabilities do you possess that might help you with the situation?

- What do you have control over in the challenge in front of you?

- How can your feelings help you problem solve the situation?

Circle the option that has the most evidence to support it. Which one seems the most believable based on the information you have right now? Write that belief on its own sheet of paper and repeat it to yourself when your old way of thinking about the situation pops into your head.

With time, you'll be able to do this internally and won't need to write down the options. You'll be able to come up with the alternatives inside your head and choose the one that makes the most sense.

Changing Self-Talk

Many of our thoughts can be considered a form of self-talk. Like other types of thoughts, self-talk has a huge impact on how we feel and act.

As you become more aware of your thoughts, you'll likely notice how much you talk to yourself. (Or is that just me?) Most people engage in self-talk throughout the day, and much of it is negative. Humans are hardwired to be critical, to judge, and to notice what's wrong or could go wrong in a situation. It makes sense when you think about cave people and how they had to enter new environments cautiously, looking for signs of danger everywhere. They also had to be critical of foods they ate to make sure they were safe, be wary of new people or creatures who might want to harm them, and just move through the world extremely carefully so they could survive. Even though we don't have the same dangers they did, our brains haven't quite caught up.

How we talk to ourselves impacts our behaviors immensely. So much, in fact, that professional athletes spend a great deal of time learning how to change their self-talk so that they perform better. In one study of 258 female gymnasts, researchers found that when the athletes engaged in positive self-talk, they performed better, and when they engaged in negative self-talk, they performed worse (Santos-Rosa et al. 2022). Basically, the gymnasts performed better when they thought something like "I'm well-prepared" versus "I want to drop out." This might sound obvious, but if you're paying attention to your thoughts, you might realize how often you engage in negative self-talk during important tasks such as taking an exam ("I'm going to fail this"), performing in front of others ("I sound dumb"), or when approaching a new group of friends ("I look so bad today"). Now you know that thinking these types of thoughts makes it more likely you'll experience negative outcomes in those situations. And now that you know this bit of information, you can flip the script!

Flipping the script and changing self-talk doesn't mean we come up with something extremely positive to say instead. In fact, doing so will make us feel even worse. If you try and say something you don't truly believe, your brain ends up trying to overcome the disbelief, resulting in you digging in your heels and believing the original thought even more. Rather, changing self-talk means coming up with something that's a bit more realistic than the original thought.

Instead of "I'm going to fail this test," you might change it to, "I've been paying attention in class and studied hard for this." Notice you didn't say "I'm going to get 100 percent" because if you don't really believe that statement, you'll now feel even more stressed than before. You just modified your self-talk statement to more accurately reflect the situation: you've been paying attention in class and you studied hard. You know this is true, so your brain doesn't have to try and overcome any sort of disbelief.

The gymnasts from the study above improved their athletic performance by changing their self-talk about the situation. You can change the outcome of your own situations by doing the same thing. Changing your self-talk might take practice, but it's completely possible, no matter how hard it feels in the beginning. Just be patient with yourself, notice your negative self-talk, write down your new self-talk statements, and choose the one that's most believable to you. The more you do it, the easier it'll get and soon, you won't need to write them down because you'll create these statements instantly and internally.

Remember how you had to come up with three to five alternatives to a situation when reframing? You can use the same number when coming up with new self-talk statements. Grab your journal and think of some negative self-talk statements you've had recently. It could be one that popped up with friends, at a club or sports event, when studying or taking a test, at work, or when trying something new. It could be a statement that occurred while you were doing something or one you thought of while preparing to do something.

- Write down a negative self-talk statement in your journal. It can be about a specific situation or a more general one about yourself.

- Create three to five new statements that are more realistic and accurately reflect the situation. (Let's say your negative self-talk statement is "I'm going to sound so bad when I present in front of the class." In coming up with new statements, you might include (1) "I've prepared really hard for this presentation"; (2) "I usually get pretty good feedback on my presentations"; (3) "I can stay focused on the material"; (4) "My parents said I sounded good when I did it for them"; (5) "I'm going to focus on the slides while I talk.")

- After considering the new statements you created, choose the option that is most accurate and the most believable to you.

- Repeat this self-talk statement over and over, write it down, make it your go-to thought for the particular situation or for yourself.

Tools for Awareness of Thoughts

Remember, awareness only gets us so far; we have to be able to regulate as well. Let's dive into some ways to practice awareness of thoughts, as well as self-regulation tools to manage the challenging ones.

Journaling: Writing about our thoughts, feelings, dreams, goals, relationships, and future is a great way to build self-awareness of our thoughts. Journaling allows for self-discovery that sticks with us longer over time than just talking through our thoughts does. Journaling is such a valuable tool that many therapists include it as "homework" for their clients.

For your journaling:

- Find a blank notebook or journal to use. It doesn't need to be anything fancy, but if you want to personalize it, go right ahead.

- Choose a time of day when you'll journal (first thing in the morning, as soon as you get home in the afternoon, right before bed…) and put the journal, or a sticky note reminding you of the journal, in a spot where you'll see it during that time. For example, if you've decided to journal first thing in the morning, put the journal right next to your alarm so you see it as soon as you wake up. Or if you have a sibling who likes to snoop, put a sticky note on your desk reminding you to journal so you know to grab it from its hidden location when you get home in the afternoon.

- Set the timer for ten minutes and write about whatever you want. For example, you can write about your day, a dream you had last night, a fight with a friend, or goals you've set for yourself. The only rule is that you're not judging yourself for what you write and you're not worrying about spelling, punctuation, or grammar.

I encourage you to journal daily. Make it a habit and a part of your daily routine. If you find that daily is too much, pick an amount of time that seems doable instead. Perhaps you journal three times a week or every Sunday night. The most important thing is that you're journaling, no matter how many or how few times in a week.

Affirmations: An affirmation is a simple statement of emotional support or encouragement. However, not all affirmations are created equally, nor do they work equally well. The trick is that you need to believe the affirmation; otherwise it'll have the opposite effect. (It's like self-talk and how we discussed that you need to change negative self-talk to statements that are more realistic and accurate, *not* ones that are overly positive and unbelievable.) For instance, if you're nervous about walking alone into a party where you barely know anyone, an affirmation of "I can get to know people while still feeling nervous" will work better than "Everyone will love me immediately" because it is more believable to your brain.

Create a list of affirmations in your journal that will encourage and support you in the coming weeks. You can make them generic so that you can use the same one for multiple situations. See if you can come up with at least five affirmations.

Logic and reasoning: This is a great one when your feelings or thoughts are easily put into words and you can clearly articulate what's going on. You know exactly what it is that's bothering you. Maybe you've just had a fight with a loved one or didn't get the job you really wanted. Or perhaps you can't decide which college to choose.

- Start off by answering the question: "What situation is upsetting/frustrating/bothering me right now?" Be specific and add details about it; however, keep it to two to three sentences.

- Next, write what feelings the situation created (use the feeling wheel if necessary).

- Write the thoughts caused by the situation. Make a list of as many as come to mind and then go through and circle one or two thoughts that are the strongest.

- Now consider the thoughts you've circled and for each one, come up with three reasons why that thought isn't true. You may have to dig deep, and if you have trouble, think of what a trusted friend, parent, therapist, coach, or teacher would come up with.

Let's consider an example. Pretend your situation is not getting the job you really wanted.

	Situation: I heard back from the store and they
	hired someone else for the spot I really wanted.

Next, you consider your feelings.

	Feelings: sad, disappointed, depressed, embarrassed,
	jealous

Now you focus on your thoughts.

	Thoughts: I must've messed up the interview.
	It's going to be so hard to tell everyone I didn't get it.
	Now I have to look for something else.
	There aren't any other jobs like this one available right now.

You consider which thoughts are the strongest and decide on two.

	Thoughts: I must've messed up the interview.
	⟨It's going to be so hard to tell everyone I didn't get it⟩
	Now I have to look for something else.
	There aren't any other jobs like this one available right now.

Now that you have your two strongest thoughts, you're going to identify three reasons why these thoughts aren't true. Let's consider just the first one for our example: "It's going to be so hard to tell everyone I didn't get it." You might come up with the first one more easily: "I know my mom will be really sympathetic about this. She knows how badly I wanted it, and she'll comfort me." However, you might find that the next two are more challenging to create. You may have to think of what your mom would even say about this. You decide on "My friends have experienced disappointment too, so they're not going to judge me" and "I don't have to announce it to the world. I can just tell those closest to me right now."

Good job building your self-awareness of thoughts and practicing these thought-based self-regulation tools! As you're working on reframing situations, changing your self-talk, and using the tools of journaling, affirmations, and logic and reasoning, be kind to yourself. Changing your thoughts takes time and you'll need to be patient with yourself. In the next chapter, we're going to focus on behaviors (woo-hoo!) so I'll meet you over there when you're ready.

CHAPTER 4

Foundational Skill: Self-Awareness of Behaviors

Self-awareness has another important component—awareness of behaviors. Self-awareness of behaviors includes not only examining our actions but also understanding the connections between our behaviors, thoughts, and emotions. As you learned in the previous chapter, our thoughts impact our feelings and behaviors. And our behaviors can impact how we feel and think. When we consider how we spend our time and how we feel and think while participating in certain activities, we're able to recognize when we need to create change. And when we understand how our small daily actions add up and impact our larger goals, we're able to see whether our daily habits are helping us move toward these goals or holding us back.

But self-awareness of behaviors also means understanding how our actions impact others and how others impact our behaviors. We're aware of what we're doing in relation to those around us and know how we might be making them feel or think. We also understand how others might be impacting our own actions.

We'll look at each of these aspects in this chapter, and by the time you're done reading it, you'll have a better understanding of what it all means and how to use self-awareness of your behaviors to create positive change in your own life.

Aligning Emotions and Behaviors

In *Love and Work*, author and researcher Marcus Buckingham (2022) writes about how crucial it is that people learn how to identify, follow, and lean into what they truly love doing. He points out that what we love makes us unique *and* leads us to a life full of connection, safety, and contribution. When we consider which of our goals light us up the most, we are figuring out which ones are most aligned with our values and desires. And when we do that, we significantly increase our chances of completing our goals.

What lights you up? Consider things you want to accomplish and the ones you get most excited about. Before you answer this question though, know that humans have the tendency to go after immediate rewards and easily forget about the big goal they truly desire. In other words, we're more likely to spend time on what feels good in the moment, like binge-watching a show, rather than focus on the smaller steps that will get us closer to the big thing we'd prefer to achieve, like getting up early to go for a run so we can complete a marathon in six months. For most of us, the immediate reward feels great in the moment, but it doesn't help us achieve the things that make us most excited.

Aligning your behaviors with your emotions is a nuanced and complex task. It's not just doing what makes you happy 100 percent of the time, but rather understanding the bigger picture and what's important to you in the long run. It's figuring out what's bringing you closer to the life you desire and what's leading you away from it. It's knowing the difference between goals you've set for yourself versus goals that have been imposed on you by parents, teachers, coaches, friends, or society. It includes being tuned into your emotions and being able to tune out the noise of the world. It takes time to be able to do this, but the more you practice what you're learning in this book, the easier it'll become.

As you examine and better understand your behaviors, I want you to consider how you *feel* during each activity. In helping people figure out what they love, Marcus Buckingham suggests keeping a "Love It/Loathe It" list where you track your daily activities and simply put each on one side of the sheet or the other (2022). So this exercise is going to have two parts, with the first one being a Love It/Loathe It list and the second part a reflection. The point of this activity is to help you figure out what you truly enjoy doing so that you can find ways to add more of what you love to your life.

Follow these steps to create your Love It/Loathe It list:

1. At the top of one sheet of paper, write Love It, and at the top of another, write Loathe It.

2. Keep these sheets with you everywhere you go for three days.

3. Track what you love doing and what you despise doing over those three days. If it's an activity that you don't feel particularly strong about one way or the other, just don't write it down.

4. At the end of each of these three days, journal and reflect on these questions:

   - Which activities energized and invigorated you today?

   - Which ones made you feel drained and like you just wasted a bunch of time?

   - Which activities did you get excited about when you thought of doing them?

   - Which ones did you dread?

   - Which activities will help you reach an important goal that you're excited about?

You might have found that there are many things on your Loathe It list that are required of you (chores, schoolwork, work), so it's important that you consider how these things tie into your bigger goals. For example, you might loathe writing college essays but going to college is important to you. Or you might loathe making your bed or doing laundry but these things tie into your desire to be responsible or to have an organized room. Connecting these types of Loathe It list items with a greater purpose or goals can help you see why they're important in the big picture of your life.

Daily Habits

Before we go any further, let's consider the story of Antonio.

Antonio is fourteen years old and just starting his summer break. During his first week, he tells his parents all about his summer plans—he wants to hang with friends at the park a lot, he really wants to learn how to do a 360 flip on his skateboard, he wants to learn Spanish, and he wants to earn some money by helping his parents and neighbors with different yard projects. However, he quickly falls into the habit of staying up late gaming and sleeping so late that he misses his friends at the park, and then has only a couple of hours to get his chores done before his parents get home from work. He still feels tired at dinner, too tired to learn Spanish or skate, and ends up getting back online to game instead. He then repeats the whole cycle again the next day. Halfway through summer break he realizes he's not doing anything he planned and feels like he's wasting his time off from school.

In *Atomic Habits*, author James Clear writes: "Success is the product of daily habits—not once-in-a-lifetime transformations" (2018). In other words, it means that it's our small daily actions that create meaningful change, help us reach our goals, or live a life we're proud of, rather than some monumental, huge event that you see in movies. We often forget this as we move through the day, but it's such an important thing to keep in mind. Our daily behaviors add up and result in a day/week/month/year we're proud of and excited about, or they add up to time we can't recall how we spent or where we wonder why we're not doing the things we set out to do.

People often complain about how they don't have time to do the things they enjoy, but when they do a time audit (where you record everything you do throughout a day and how much time you spend on each thing), they quickly realize how much time they're spending on time-sucks. Time-sucks are activities or relationships that quickly eat up our time while not adding any value to our lives. It's so easy to engage in time-sucks and to find ourselves at the end of the day with the realization that we didn't do a single thing we truly enjoyed or needed to do.

I once had a teen complain to me about not having any time for friends because of homework, but when she did a time audit, she found that she spent only sixty minutes a day on homework and five hours on her phone every day after school! She genuinely thought all her time was going to homework and was shocked at how much time she spent scrolling social media and watching videos about things she couldn't even recall later. And you know what? Her experience is extremely common.

As humans, we're notoriously bad at understanding how we spend our time and at estimating how long we think things will take. This isn't a teen or young adult thing; this is a human thing. We all have *cognitive biases* that make us bad with time. A cognitive bias is a mental shortcut that impacts our memory, how we perceive things, how we reason, and how we act. A cognitive bias isn't based in fact but rather personal experience and, therefore, likely incorrect. For example, due to some of the cognitive biases humans have, we think that some things are more urgent than they really are, that things will take less time than they actually will, and that an immediate reward is better than something that will benefit us in the future.

Like Antonio did initially, it's so easy to fall into a routine full of immediate rewards but lacking anything that will add up to something substantial. Therefore, paying attention to time-sucks and emotions is so important, as doing so will help you avoid that trap. We all have habits, some healthy and some not so healthy, but as you become more self-aware of your behaviors, you'll notice which ones are hurting you and you can start to create positive change. You're going to do a time audit in just a bit to help you identify your daily habits, activities, and time-sucks.

Perhaps you're unsure of what healthy habits even are. Well, let's do a little review. You might recall reading in the introduction about the group of Australian researchers who identified a "mental vaccine" that consists of habits that promote stress-resilience, well-being, and learning. This vaccine is made up of healthy eating, physical activity, rest and sleep, optimism, variety and challenge, social interactions with friends, learning new things, repetition, managing stress, and making autonomous decisions (Ekman et al. 2021).

As you're identifying what healthy habits you need to incorporate into your own life, it'll be helpful to know how to get yourself to do them. Multiple studies have demonstrated that adolescents aged thirteen to seventeen years are more motivated by rewards and incentives than other age-groups (Casey, Duhoux, and Cohen 2010). If you fall in that range, figure out some rewards or incentives to get you going. The trick is that your rewards shouldn't fall under the unhealthy habit or time-suck categories because, if they do, you're just setting yourself up for failure.

Think about it for a moment—you're trying to increase the amount of exercise you get each day and use watching YouTube as a reward. So you get in your daily walk and come home and start watching videos, which you know is hard to stop. You end up starting your homework late, skip dinner, and go to bed way past when you should. The next day after school, you're too tired to go on your daily walk…

See how quickly we can get off track? Instead, create rewards or incentives that foster other healthy habits. Perhaps you tell your friends that if you go on a daily walk this week, you'll host a movie night with them (remember how real-life social interactions are part of the mental vaccine?). You can also include things you love in order to incentivize yourself. Maybe you love dogs, so you ask the neighbor if you can walk his each day, or you include the local dog park on your route so you can watch them play for a bit before heading home. Get creative and have fun with your habits so you're more likely to stick with them.

Part 1

Take a moment to reflect on how you spend your time and think back to the Love It/ Loathe It exercise. Do you think you spend your time mostly on things you enjoy? Or do you think you waste a lot of your time? Perhaps you feel much of your time is spent on things you *have* to do rather than things you *want* to do.

For this exercise, don't go back through your planner, phone, calendar, or screen use app. Just use your journal to write from memory about how you spend your time.

- In your journal, create different categories that represent the bulk of time in your schedule, like school, homework, studying, work, friends, gaming, scrolling, videos (movies, TV, YouTube), family, exercise, and clubs.

- Under each category, estimate how much time a day you spend in that area.

- Now go back through and add an estimate of how much time a week you spend in that area.

- Finally, look through your list and circle any activity that you truly enjoyed doing. Perhaps this activity energized and invigorated you, or you got excited about doing it before you even started, or it's helping you reach an important goal you're excited about.

Now that you've created daily and weekly estimates for each important category in your life, we're going to see how accurate you were.

Part 2

Do a time audit on three different days. Choose days that are typical for you, not days when you're doing something completely new or out of the ordinary.

- Carry your journal, a small notebook, or a piece of paper with you everywhere you go on these three days and record every activity you do as soon as you start it, along with the time you began.

- **Note**: *Please do not use your phone for this exercise! Our phones are designed to be distracting, and they're really good at it. If you use your phone to record your time, you'll undoubtedly get pulled into something else and forget to make your recording. Seriously. Don't even try it! I've been through this with way too many clients to know that even if you think you're the one who can fight the distraction urge, you're not. Trust me. I'm not the one either. I've yet to meet the one.*

- Once you're done, just write down the end time. Don't add up numbers or pay attention to what you're recording; just go about your day like normal.

- No judging, looking through your list, or criticizing; you're just collecting data.

- At the end of the day, just before lights out, go through and add up how much time you spent on each activity.

- Create categories like those you made during part 1 of this exercise (school, homework, studying, work, friends, gaming, scrolling, videos, family, exercise, clubs) and enter the total time for that day in each one.

Once you've completed the time audit on three different days, look back at part 1, where you estimated how much time you spent in different areas and compare. Use your journal to answer these questions:

- How far off were your estimates?

- Which categories were you better at estimating your time in? Why do you think that is?

- Which categories were hard to be accurate in? Why do you think that is?

- How much time is spent on time-sucks?

- How much time is spent on activities that energize you versus activities that drain you?

- How much time is spent on activities that you get excited about doing?

- How much time is spent on activities that are bringing you closer to a goal you're excited about?

- Which areas would you like to see change in on how much or how little time is spent?

- What do you think you could do differently starting tomorrow?

The Impact of Change

Now let's pretend that Antonio has been working on his emotional intelligence. He understands the importance of self-awareness when it comes to following through on things. He knows that he must pay attention to how he feels to make sure his goals are truly aligned with what he wants (self-awareness of emotions). He also understands that he needs to examine how he spends his time and assess whether that is bringing him closer to or further from his goals (self-awareness of behaviors). Let's rewrite his story to reflect his growth.

Antonio is fourteen years old and just starting his summer break. During his first week, he tells his parents all about his summer plans—he wants to hang with friends at the park a lot, he really wants to learn how to do a 360 flip on his skateboard, he wants to learn Spanish, and he wants to earn some money by helping his parents and neighbors with different yard projects. He *considers how excited* he is about each goal and then he *prioritizes*, deciding that earning money is his top priority, landing a 360 flip is next, hanging with friends is third, and learning Spanish is last. He uses his priority list to *map out* when he'll work on each goal and sets deadlines for when he hopes to achieve each. He considers what might take him away from reaching his goals (video games, videos, and a particular friend who just likes to complain all the time) and *sets limits* on how long he can spend doing those things each day. He even decides how he'll *reward* himself once he's earned a certain amount of money and landed the skate trick.

How might Antonio's summer change now that he's aware of how important his goals are? What might he do differently now that he's made plans on how to execute his goals? How differently will he spend his time now that he's identified what's taking him away from his goals and set time limits on those activities? Think of how he'll feel halfway through the summer now. (And take special note of the italicized words; you're going to learn how to do each of them when we get into goal-setting strategies later in this chapter.)

When we're practicing self-awareness of our behaviors, we're aware of how we're spending our time, including time on things we're not particularly proud of or don't even want to be doing. We accurately assess how we're spending our time to make changes so that we're doing things that are truly aligned with our goals, joys, or life vision. It sounds so simple, but if you're someone who often feels overwhelmed and stressed or that you're not doing things that are important to you, you know how hard this task really is.

Our Behaviors and Others

Understanding our own behaviors isn't just about us; we need to also consider how our actions impact others and how others impact our behaviors. Humans are social creatures after all. We rely on one another to survive, and we impact each other quite a bit, whether we mean to or not. Let's consider for a moment how we interact with other people and how we impact them with our own behaviors by looking at Mason's story.

Mason didn't sleep well last night. In fact, he barely slept at all. He got caught up texting with friends about some big relationship drama going on within his friend group and completely lost track of time. When he hears his mom calling to wake him up, he notices that she sounds really angry. He looks at the clock and sees how late he is, and he realizes she's likely been trying to wake him for a while. He also remembers how she asked him to be on time this morning for reasons he can't quite recall—he just knows it was really important. Oops! He rushes downstairs, dressed in dirty clothes from the floor, and without having showered. His mom looks him over, sighs, and says, "If that's how you want to show up today, I'm not gonna stop you. Now hurry up, you have to drop your sister off on your way in today and she can't be late. She has orchestra auditions. And I have a huge meeting to get to." Crap, now he remembers! His little sister is already waiting in the car, chewing her fingernails and with tears in her eyes. He knows her well enough to recognize that she's anxious, so he tries to reassure her: "I'm gonna get you there on time, stop freaking out!" She doesn't say anything and just sits quietly during the whole ride, clutching her viola case to her chest and checking the clock every other minute. When he drops her off, she goes running into the building, and he feels awful that he made her late on such a special day.

How do you think Mason's behavior impacted his mom? How did it impact his little sister? What do you think their days are going to be like now? If Mason had completed the first exercise in this chapter and identified that helping around the house is tied into his overall value of wanting to be more responsible, how do you think he would feel in not honoring one of his values?

But it's not just our behavior impacting others like we saw with Mason. Our own feelings are also impacted by those around us. On NPR's *Morning Edition*, correspondent Allison Aubrey (2019) reported on research done by Yale University sociologist Nicholas Christakis. This research has shown that emotions spread through social networks. For example, we have a 25 percent higher chance of being happier if those in our home and immediate life are happy with their own lives. In contrast, anger and sadness in those around us can make us feel angry and sad too. If you're working as a cashier and interact with a frustrated customer, for instance, you're more likely to leave the situation feeling frustrated. But the real kicker of it all is, we're usually unaware of how affected we are by the positive and negative emotions of others. It happens on a subconscious level and is called *emotional contagion*.

Emotional contagion doesn't just show up in real life or immediate interactions, though. Dr. Christakis also documented how emotions spread through digital networks. If we text a friend living across the country a message conveying sadness, that friend is more likely to also feel sad now. And if we see angry posts on social media, even if we don't know the person who posted directly, we're more likely to feel angry ourselves. We're directly affected by what we see online, even if we don't know the content creator or won't be directly impacted by the information they're sharing. We mirror their emotions, and our emotional state changes, whether we're aware of it or not.

The research mentioned above demonstrates how emotions spread through digital networks. We also know that adolescents ages thirteen to eighteen now spend an hour and a half a day using social media, which is a lot of time when you think about all your other responsibilities (Rideout et al. 2022). Given these two things, I'm going to have you do a social media cleanse. You've heard of cleanses before, right? Usually, people do them with food, eliminating certain types from their diet to see how they feel. Well, we're going to do the same sort of thing, just with social media accounts and platforms. When we change or eliminate things that aren't aligned with our values and goals, we're better able to focus on the things that are.

In just a moment, you'll get a chance to go through your most used social media platforms and clean them up a bit, but before you do, I want you to take a few minutes to journal.

- List your most used social media platforms and leave space next to each one.

- In the space next to each one, write an *estimate* of how long you spend each day on that specific platform.

- Now take a quick look at your screen time over the past week, and write down how long you've *actually* spent on each one. (You might need to search how to do this, depending on what kind of phone you have.)

- For each social media platform, write down your reason for using that particular app. Is it for connection? To learn? To be entertained? To create your own content? To be inspired or motivated? To keep up with trends, fashion, gossip? For work? To see what an ex is up to (be honest!)? If there's more than one reason, write them all down. And it's okay if you use the same reasons for different apps. For example, you might use both Snapchat and Instagram for connection and entertainment.

- Consider how your different reasons make you feel. Which reasons are good for your mental health? Which ones are harming it? What changes do you need to make? For example, if you're using Instagram only to keep up with an ex and to know the latest gossip, maybe you need to either delete the app or change your reasons for using it. Perhaps instead you decide to use Instagram to be inspired. Make the change on your list.

- Now you're going to go into each app one by one. Let's start with your most used platform. Look at your reasons for using that one. Set your timer for ten minutes and get to work cleaning it up—anything that doesn't fall under your reason for being on that app gets muted, unfollowed, or deleted. Suppose you're using TikTok for motivation in your sport. You'll want to get rid of accounts that aren't athletes or coaches in your sport. You likely won't get through your whole feed or all the accounts you follow in ten minutes, and that's fine. Once your timer goes off, go to the next most used platform, review your reasons for being on it, set the timer for another ten minutes, and delete accounts that don't fit. And then go on to the next until you've cleaned up all your social media platforms.

The next time you're on each account, keep in mind your reasons for using it so you can continue cleaning as you scroll. Eventually, you'll be following only the accounts you truly want to be on.

When we rewrote Antonio's story, you might recall some italicized words. These words are important in setting and reaching goals—consider emotions, prioritize, map it out, set limits on time-sucks/barriers, and rewards. For Antonio, more awareness of his behaviors helped him better reach his goals.

Goal Setting

Time to do a deep dive into how this might look for you. Consider what you wrote down in the previous exercises regarding your loves and loathes, and think about how you're impacted by others (think of emotional contagion). Also consider your time audit and social media cleanse. All this information will ensure that you're creating goals that fit you.

Before you read through the sections below, write out your own list of goals. Take time to create a list of things you want to achieve in the next six to twelve months. Then you can apply each section to your own list.

Considering Your Emotions

People, especially adolescents, tend to do what others think they should be doing and then set goals accordingly. Parents tell you which college is best for you, friends tell you who you should date, coaches tell you what your strengths and weaknesses are, teachers tell you what you should study, and society tells you what's acceptable for your age, gender identity, race, ethnicity, body type, and so on. While some of this might be extremely useful feedback that will help you grow, some of it is absolutely useless.

You and *only* you know how you feel about your goals. If you set goals that are aligned with what others think you should be doing but that don't resonate or align with how you feel, the goals will be exhausting (in a bad way) and extremely difficult to achieve. However, if you set goals that light you up, you won't care how exhausting they are or how hard they might be to achieve because they will energize and drive you (this is exhaustion in a good way). When you create your goals, consider your emotions and identify the goal you can't wait to achieve. When you imagine that you've reached each of your listed goals, which one do you want to scream to the world "I did it!" and dance and jump around about?

Prioritizing Your Goals

Number your list in order, starting with the one you're most excited about. Don't worry about how unrealistic it might feel or all the steps it'll take to get there—you're ranking these goals by emotional reaction, not by anything else.

I know, I know, you're saying that it's impossible, that there are too many steps, or that your goal is too big. But that's not what we're focusing on right now. We're focusing on putting them in order from the one that lights you up the most on down. We'll worry about all the work in the next step, but for now, this is all about alignment. Aligning your goals with your emotions. Because if you're not excited to achieve them, what's the point?

Mapping Out Your Goals

This is probably the most time-consuming step and the one you'll revisit and rework again and again. Mapping out goals includes writing out each step, no matter how small or insignificant it seems; setting deadlines for each one; and entering due dates into calendars or planners. Some adolescents like to skip this mapping step (ahem, ahem), but please don't! Without it, you're just a boat drifting without a sail, with no direction or way to keep you on course. You won't reach your destination, you'll become frustrated, and you'll be less likely to set future goals. Instead, take control of your destination by figuring out your course ahead of time.

Let's see what this might look like. Pretend that your top goal is to get an internship at a veterinary clinic. First, list the steps on paper. What are the vet clinic's requirements for interns? Perhaps you learn that you need a certain GPA, volunteer experience, and the ability to handle challenging animals. Write each one down. Next, figure out what you need for each of these specific requirements and create a list that includes any materials or help from others. Maybe your GPA isn't quite what it needs to be, so you list joining a study group, finding a tutor, and spending more time on schoolwork. Let's say you already have volunteer experience, so you can cross that requirement off the list; however, you don't have experience handling challenging animals. You decide to contact the local animal shelter to see if you can gain some experience there. Next, set dates for when you can achieve each step. Look at the list of what you need to do (joining study group, hiring tutor, more time on schoolwork, and contacting animal shelter) and figure out when you can do each. For example, when will you attend study groups or meet with a tutor? Where in your calendar can you fit more studying? When will you call the animal shelter? And finally, put your tasks on your calendar and set reminders on your devices. Cross them off as you complete them or move them to another time on the calendar if necessary.

This graphic shows the steps that you can follow for your own goals.

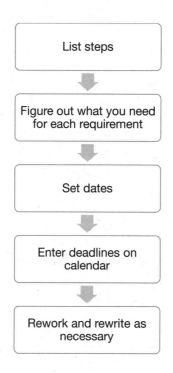

Setting Limits

Remember how Antonio considered what might take him away from reaching his goals and set limits on how long he could spend doing those things each day? What are the things that take you off track? What are your time-sucks? What do you find yourself consistently getting distracted by? These are your barriers to reaching your goals, and you need to know what they are so you can stop them before they start to impact your progress. For Antonio, it was video games, videos, and a particular friend who just likes to complain all the time. For me, it's scrolling mindlessly on social media and certain Netflix shows.

Once you've identified your time-sucks/barriers, schedule in when you're allowed to engage in the activity and set a time limit. This might mean putting off the time-suck until later in the day because you know how hard it is to stop. Or you may have to ask a family member to remind you if they find you binge-watching a show rather than turning it off after one episode. If it's particularly hard for you to stop, you may have to eliminate the barrier altogether by asking your parents or roommates to change the Netflix password or by deleting the social media app from your phone. If you have a friend who tends to take you off track, you might need to ignore texts or DMs, hang out with them in groups instead of alone, or limit your interactions to weekly instead of daily.

Choosing Your Rewards

You already learned what makes a helpful reward versus an unhelpful one, so now's the time to create a list that you can choose from as needed. You might have larger rewards that you can attach to the more difficult-to-achieve deadlines and smaller ones for the easier steps. I find that eating squares of dark chocolate is a great reward for getting through smaller steps, but I need an oat milk latte for the bigger ones. Play around with what incentivizes you and see what works best for you.

Whew! You did *a lot* of work in this chapter. You analyzed your behaviors, aligned emotions and actions, closely examined how you spend your time, did a social media cleanse, and learned how to set goals. You also considered how your behavior affects others *and* how your behavior is affected by others. Take some time to digest the material, apply it to your life, and I'll see you in just a bit.

Oh, wait... Remember the earlier mention of vibe checks, sections designed to help you stay on track with your goals? You're going to see Vibe Check Your Goals sections after the remaining chapters, so keep your goal list close. You'll be revisiting it often.

CHAPTER 5

Foundational Skill: Self-Regulation

So far in this book, you've been building your self-awareness. You're likely more aware of your emotions, thoughts, and behaviors, and hopefully you've been increasing your awareness more and more each day through reflections and journaling, and by practicing some of the exercises from this book. But there's something you need to know—when people have too much self-awareness and lack self-regulation skills, they tend to ruminate (get stuck on negative thoughts), feel more physical symptoms of stress, and have lower self-confidence. In contrast, when people have emotional awareness *and* are skilled at self-regulating, they rebound quicker from stressful events, have fewer physical symptoms of stress, and quickly move on from negative thoughts (Salovey et al. 2002). Basically, self-awareness on its own can actually make you feel worse, but when it's paired with self-regulation, you'll be prepared to deal with whatever life throws at you.

We touched on self-regulation tools in the previous chapters, and we're going to use this chapter to really get into them. And just a heads-up—there's a lot of information to digest in here, so be sure to take breaks when you're overwhelmed or tired or notice you're no longer absorbing the content. We're going to discuss what it means to be dysregulated, how to identify dysregulation when it's happening to you, whether venting helps with regulation, self-regulation tools, and how to build resilience. Self-awareness is only as helpful as your ability to deal with emotions that being more aware brings up, so we need to spend some time here to make sure you know what to do. Let's get started.

Teens and young adults sometimes rely on passive coping tools to self-regulate. Passive coping tools are considered less helpful and refer to avoiding and giving up. These tools include alcohol, marijuana, or other substances. They can also include phones, computers, gaming, social media, gambling, or other internet or technological devices that are used to avoid emotional distress or to distract from the discomfort that accompanies situations or emotions. Using passive tools provides temporary relief and might even increase pleasant feelings and relaxation momentarily; however, they lead to a tricky road ahead. Passive tools end up making the emotional discomfort stronger once the temporary relief is up, because they deny you the opportunity to deal with the distress you are feeling and manage it in a way that improves the stressful situation. As a result, you are more likely to use another passive tool, and round and round you go.

On the flip side, active coping tools are considered more helpful and include steps we take to feel better in a stressful situation. Active coping tools include the self-regulation tools covered in chapters 1 (feeling labeling, taking a break, mindfulness), 2 (rhythmic movement, paced breathing), and 3 (journaling, affirmations, logic and reasoning) as well as what you'll learn in this chapter. When we use an active tool to manage emotional distress, discomfort, or stress, we learn that we can go outside our comfort zone, that we can handle hard situations, and that we can improve our internal and external states. Active tools empower us and allow us to change our circumstances, emotions, moods, relationships, and perspective. Imagine being able to calmly respond to a boss's criticism about your work performance or realizing that a low score on a test isn't the end of the world. When we don't allow people around us or our current environment to dictate how we feel, think, or act, we're in control and we have the power. That's a pretty big deal.

Signs of Dysregulation

Dysregulation is a severe emotional response to a situation. It's more than making a sarcastic comment when a friend teases you, it's yelling at them. It's not just feeling disappointed when a potential date turns you down, it's throwing things. Some people describe dysregulation as being moody or having mood swings. This can look like dramatic changes in your mood, like going from being depressed for most of the day to being anxious in the evening to being angry at bedtime. Or dysregulation might look like a constant array of emotional outbursts, such as snapping at friends because you're irritated, sobbing because you're overwhelmed, and spam-texting your partner because you're insecure. Being dysregulated can make you feel out of control and interfere with your relationships, school, work, and how you feel about yourself. Dysregulation can look like you're all over the place with your emotions— yelling, crying, and fighting with friends and family members. It can also feel scary, with thoughts of suicide or doing things to hurt yourself (De Berardis et al. 2020).

It can be difficult to know whether your emotional response to a difficult situation is considered more extreme than typical. Sometimes you must rely on how others perceive or respond to you or what trusted individuals tell you. Let's say you just found out that you didn't get into your top choice of college, and you respond by crying, screaming at your parents, blaming your teachers, and running into your bedroom, where you slam the door and sob on the bed. Your parents give you some time to cool off and then come check on you, finding that you're now under the covers, scrolling on your phone, and saying that you're not going to college anymore. If they're parents who understand emotional awareness and self-regulation, they'll likely tell you that this is an extreme emotional response and that you need to find another way to cope with the bad news. They might even suggest that you go for a run, do some yoga, take a bubble bath, or listen to music.

If you trust your parents, you'll understand that you're in a state of dysregulation and that you need to self-regulate in a healthy, active way. You might decide to engage in one of the tools they suggested, which will help you calm down and form a new perspective on the situation. With time, you'll realize that while it's a total bummer you didn't get your top pick, there are other colleges available to you. You'll also likely see that a dysregulated response doesn't help the situation and, in fact, makes everything worse.

Another way to determine whether your emotional response is extreme or typical is by considering how your response impacts important areas of your life. Pretend that your manager at the restaurant where you work just denied your requested day off for later this week, a day when you'd planned to go to the beach with a group of friends. You need this job badly and can't afford to lose it; however, you find yourself storming around the restaurant and gossiping with coworkers about how bad the manager is at their job. You quickly realize though that your behavior could have a negative impact on your job, meaning that your emotional response is extreme. You realize that you need to self-regulate. You go into the bathroom for a break, where you practice paced breathing and engage in helpful self-talk. You're still annoyed that you'll miss the beach day but you're relieved that you recognized signs of dysregulation early enough to intervene.

Dysregulation sounds like a scary thing to experience, but it's far more common than you might think. Most teens and young adults experience dysregulation from time to time, but we all have different factors that make us more likely to tip over from a normal reaction to dysregulation. For example, some of us are really sensitive to our environment, meaning that changes in noise levels or temperature prove particularly challenging. Others might be sensitive to their internal state or relationships, meaning irritability or an argument with a friend evokes dysregulation. Regardless, teens and young adults are more impulsive than adults (due to their maturing *prefrontal cortex*—the part of the brain that helps with impulse control), which means that they are currently more disposed to dysregulation than they will be later in life (Young, Sandman, and Craske 2019). Moreover, while it's common for you to experience emotional dysregulation, you're more likely to develop anxiety and depression if you don't know how to regulate the extreme emotions.

Break It Down

Let's look at the signs of dysregulation a little more closely so that you can determine for yourself when you're entering this challenging state of mind.

- Angry outbursts include yelling, screaming, hitting, punching, kicking, or destroying property. They can also include saying cruel things to others.

- Uncontrollable crying is when you find that you can't stop crying or are heaving so hard that you make yourself sick.

- Fights with friends and family members, especially when unprovoked, can be a big indicator of dysregulation. Other times, you might find that they said or did something that would make anyone feel upset; however, your reaction is more intense than the original situation.

- Suicidal thoughts include thoughts of wanting to die or that the world/people/situation would be better off without you.

- Self-harming behaviors are physically harmful things people sometimes do to themselves that cause immediate pain.

- Rigidity or inflexibility looks like difficulty adapting to change or transition. It can also look like perfectionism or trouble thinking in new ways.

- An inability to care for oneself occurs when you can't take care of personal hygiene like brushing teeth, showering, or changing into clean clothes. It can also include not eating throughout the day or eating only junk food as well as sleeping too much or too little.

- Food restricting is when a person limits their food intake without the guidance or recommendation of a health professional, and binge eating is when a person overconsumes food to the point of vomiting.

- Substance use and/or abuse includes marijuana, alcohol, or other drugs. It also includes taking prescription drugs not as prescribed by your doctor.

- Constant irritability looks like being grumpy all the time, feeling on edge or tense, or ready to snap at the smallest inconvenience or upset.

To Vent or Not

Sharing our emotions, or venting, with others can be a great thing. It can help us feel connected to those we vent to or with, it can help us identify and process our emotions, and it can help us think differently about a situation (Suttie 2021). For example, venting with peers about the difficulty of a test can create a sense of belonging, help you move through feelings of anxiety about your performance, and even make you feel better to learn that it was a struggle for most of your class. Thinking differently about a situation (reframing) can be observed when we find humor or purpose in a difficult time. When we share our emotions with skilled listeners, venting can be beneficial and help with self-regulation.

However, research shows that too much venting can make us feel worse. Sometimes people only want to vent, which turns into complaining, and never move out of this phase. Too much time spent talking about a negative experience isn't helpful because it keeps you stuck there. You're unable to move into problem solving or to reframe how you think about the experience. You're ruminating (stuck on negative thoughts) and will continue to experience emotional distress.

In addition, sharing with those who don't know how to respond can also make us feel worse. Others might also start to vent or complain about a similar situation, reinforcing the belief that things are as awful as you think they are. Or they might jump right into problem solving, causing you to feel as though your feelings aren't valid. And if you vent often, friends and family members may get irritated and avoid spending time with you (Parlamis 2012).

To get the benefits of venting while staying away from the negative effects, limit the amount of time you allow yourself to vent, choose who you vent to wisely, and make sure you're not constantly venting throughout the day. When it comes to limiting the amount of time to vent, even if it's private and in a journal, I encourage my clients to set a timer for three to five minutes and to keep their venting contained within that time frame. When choosing who to vent to, consider whether it's someone who can listen and validate your feelings or someone who tends to go straight to problem solving. Consider whether the person joins in on your venting, turning the conversation into a total complaint session, or if they help you find purpose, humor, or another perspective. Finally, keep tabs on how often you feel the need to vent in a day. If you find that you're venting more than once a day, it looks like you need to work on finding other self-regulation tools.

Choosing a Coping Tool

We all have our own preferred methods of distraction, and we tend to gravitate toward some healthy coping mechanisms more than others. And please don't be fooled by the term "healthy coping mechanisms." While the term sounds clinical and boring, they actually can be things you truly enjoy doing. For instance, while being in nature is one of the tools listed below, you might love hiking so much that you naturally want to do it, regardless of your current mental state.

And for the healthy self-regulation tools that take a bit more effort to use, they will get easier with time and become more natural. Think back to when you started a new job or semester and had to wake up earlier than you were used to. For the first couple of weeks, the alarm jarred you awake, and it was hard to roll out of bed. But then something shifted and you started to wake up with the alarm, not because of it. And perhaps, eventually, you started to wake up before the alarm—if it even went off at all. As humans, we take time to adjust to new things, but once we do, the new thing becomes the old thing that we now do naturally.

The following coping tools can be added to your growing list. These are three new ones that can help you feel more in control of your emotions and actions, whether you're fully dysregulated or not.

Letting it go: Sometimes all we can do is let it go. Coach is unfairly playing others more than you, a teacher grades way too harshly, or your parents have rules that are much stricter than your friends' parents. Or maybe it's a situation where you've tried to problem solve or talk it out, but there's nothing that can be done about it. In these situations, we must let it go. Saying that we'll let something go is very different from letting it go. When we truly let go of a situation or feeling, we're no longer talking or thinking about it. We're not focused on problem solving anymore. We're not complaining to friends about it. The situation or feeling is no longer part of our life. To become skilled at letting go, practice with small feelings or situations—things where you don't care too much so it's easy to let them go. The more skilled you become with the smaller things, the easier it'll be to use this tool with the larger feelings or situations. Here are three different ways to let go of hard things:

- Visualize putting the situation into a hot air balloon and watching it float away into the clouds. Really imagine it. Take time to figure out the color patterns of the balloon, the way the sky looks, the area around the balloon as it takes off. Imagine putting your situation or feeling into the balloon, and perhaps even saying good-bye to it. As it starts to drift away, imagine the weight of the feeling or situation leaving you as well. You now feel lighter. Wave to the balloon as it gets farther and farther away.

- Let go through your body by inhaling peace and exhaling the issue. Sit quietly and visualize peace and calm entering your nose with every inhale and the feeling from the situation leaving your body through your mouth with every exhale. You can even push the feeling or situation out harder on the exhales by acting as though you're blowing out candles. Make the inhales last around four seconds and the exhales around six seconds. Inhale peace and exhale the issue about five times each, with the final exhale being your largest push. Once you've completed the final exhale, tell yourself that you're done with the situation and moving on, and get up and continue with your day.

- Journal about why and how you'll let it go. Set a timer for five minutes and write about why you're letting go and how you plan to do it. Write about the benefits of letting go and how you think you'll feel once you've done it. Write about what you'll do later that day once you've let go and moved on. If you find that you don't need the full five minutes and that you let go before the timer went off, congratulations! But if you're still furiously scribbling when the timer goes off, slam that journal shut immediately, tell yourself you're officially done, and go find something productive to do.

The key is that once you've decided to let something go and visualized, exhaled, or written it away, you now must let it go. No more venting and no more thinking about it. Consider it gone. And remember to practice with easy things to let go of so that you've got the skill set in place for the bigger and harder situations and feelings.

Being in nature: Depending on where you live, you'll need to modify this one. It's not likely that you're living in a forest without another house in sight. But if you are, you know how powerful time in nature can be. It relaxes, refreshes, and rejuvenates us all at once. However, even if you live in a city, nature can still be found in parks, yards, or the open sky.

Even looking at pictures or listening to sounds of nature helps relax people while also improving attention and concentration. Being in nature can also help people gain a new perspective and feel more connected to the world around them (Weir 2020). These benefits can come from staring at the sky to watch clouds or stars, looking at trees and flowers in a nearby park, walking around your own backyard to find insects to watch, or going to a local lake or forest preserve to explore.

Use nature as a self-regulation tool and try different forms.

- Go for a hike when you feel dysregulated and see how you feel afterward.

- Pause and look at the stars before entering your home at night and notice if it causes any shift in mood.

- Find a favorite outdoor spot, whether at the beach or a park bench on a busy sidewalk where you get a view of clouds, and use it when you need to relax or calm your mind.

No matter how you use nature to self-regulate, just make sure that you're engaging with it while you're in it. This means practicing mindfulness—focusing on the sights, sounds, smells, textures, and even tastes. It also means noticing things about the sky, trees, insects, plants, or ground by paying attention to what's around you. You're not going for a hike while vent-texting a friend so that you can't even remember if you passed a flower when you're done. You're not staring at the sky while thinking about the situation. You're actively engaging with your senses, and you're present in the experience.

Recalling happy memories: Think of a happy memory. It can be a vacation you went on with your family, a concert you went to with a friend, or the time you drove by yourself for the first time and felt absolute freedom. Try and recall as many details as possible with as many senses as you can:

- What do you see in this memory?
- What sounds do you hear?
- Is there a smell?
- What's the temperature of the air or the feeling of any materials near you?
- Is there a taste?

The more senses you engage, the better. Practice pulling this happy memory up and add more detail to it each time. The more you do it, the easier it'll be to put yourself there when you really need a mental escape.

Gratitude

Dr. Robert Emmons has spent over two decades researching gratitude and has found many benefits of regularly engaging in the practice. Did you know that our brains cannot process gratitude and envy at the same time? We also can't feel gratitude and resentment simultaneously. When we're grateful, we're focused on what we have, not what we don't. Additionally, when we feel gratitude, our brains release dopamine and serotonin, biochemicals that make us feel lighter and happier. Dr. Emmons says that we can create more gratitude in our lives, no matter our circumstances, by switching our focus (Emmons 2013).

Grab your journal and sit in a quiet place where you're not likely to be disturbed. Christopher Littlefield, who trains business leaders on how to appreciate their workers (2020), suggests taking time to answer these gratitude-boosting questions:

- What did I see today that was beautiful, kind, or surprising in a good way?

- What are some opportunities I've had over the last month that I'm grateful for?

- What am I better at today than I was a year ago?

Notice how you feel now that you've spent time reflecting on these questions. How has your mood shifted? How have your thoughts changed? Keep these questions someplace where you can easily find them so you can use them when feeling envious, jealous, or resentful.

Emotional Intelligence and Resilience

Difficult experiences are a part of life. We lose loved ones, our parents divorce, we must move from a town where we know everyone to a place where we know no one. Some people cope with adverse experiences better than others though. For some individuals, hard experiences cause a system shutdown, and they no longer participate in life the way they did prior to the experience. For others, difficult experiences create disruption and upset; however, they're able to adapt. People who can adapt are considered resilient. No matter how you deal with difficult experiences though, you can grow. If you're someone who experiences a system shutdown, this book is here to help you. And if you think you're pretty adaptable and resilient, the skills you'll learn will keep you moving and developing on that path.

Researchers have found that people who are high in emotional intelligence adapt more easily to negative life experiences. Thus, emotionally intelligent people are considered more resilient. Think about why for a moment. If you're able to understand your emotions, can communicate them effectively, and know how to self-regulate, you're going to be able to handle stressful situations pretty well, don't you think? The researchers just mentioned agreed and took it one step further. In a study of over four hundred participants, they broke down the components that make up emotional intelligence. They found that when people are aware of their own emotions, can express them effectively, have control over them, and can change a negative mood into a positive one, they are significantly more resilient to negative life events (Armstrong, Galligan, and Critchley 2011).

This finding is a big one. It means that when awful things happen, we can bounce back. I'm not talking about toxic positivity and saying you should put on a happy face and instantly start talking about the good things that came out of your bad situation. Toxic positivity is not healthy or helpful, as it can cause us to suppress or avoid emotions. But instead, you decide that these bad situations won't take control of you or define who you are, what you do, and how you live.

You've been building awareness of your emotions while reading this book. You've also been working on effectively expressing them and learning how to have control over your emotions. We'll focus on being resilient in tough times in this section. You'll have the skill set to be more resilient so you can handle whatever negative life experiences cross your path.

Tools to Build Resilience

Exercising: There's now so much research on how exercise decreases stress, depression, and anxiety that it's completely old news. Exercise creates new pathways in our brains, which makes us feel and think differently. It acts as a preventive aid to stave off irritability, sadness, lethargy, and apathy, *and* it immediately changes our mood during difficult times.

Exercise will leave us more prepared to deal with difficult events when they inevitably do happen if we use it as an overall mood manager. To do this, exercise forty-five to sixty minutes a day, five days a week. The key to it helping mental health is that it needs to be at least moderate, which means causing an elevated heart rate. You should be out of breath while doing it. It doesn't matter what kind of exercise you're doing—dancing, swimming, running, kayaking, volleyball, biking, karate, weight training, soccer, or skating. It just needs to get your heart rate going and you should be sweating.

Make exercise part of your daily routine. Think of it like taking a multivitamin. You take a vitamin to keep your immune system strong and stave off sickness. Exercise is a vitamin for your mood. You're doing it to keep your mental health strong and to help you better handle stress and mood dysregulation.

To use exercise as an immediate mood changer during stressful or difficult times, do ten minutes of intense exercise as soon as you feel in distress. Your heart rate needs to be elevated and you need to work up a good sweat, so it should be something difficult for you, like running, burpees, or jumping rope. All you have to do is set the timer and start. These ten minutes will cause a release of endorphins in your brain that will create an immediate shift in how you feel and think.

Listening to music: Music can evoke changes in important systems within our brains. A researcher at the University of Bergen, Norway, used brain imaging to see how listening to music affects the brain and found that numerous brain structures involved with emotion are significantly impacted by listening to music. Not only can music create strong emotions or strong actions (like dancing or moving), it changes our physiological activity and can reduce or speed up heart rates. Music can also create connection or social belongingness—just think of a concert you attended where everyone was grooving together or a time when you were singing along to a favorite song with a group of people (Koelsch 2018).

Create playlists of music for different moods. What music tends to make you feel better, get you moving, or feel connected to others? Put it on your list. Create several different playlists for different moods. I have a client who has her "Move Yo' Body" playlist filled with energizing songs that make her want to run, a "Stop the Funk" playlist of upbeat and optimistic songs to help with feelings of depression and sadness, and a "Sis...Really?" compilation of protest songs for social justice that help when she feels overwhelmed with current events.

Getting creative: Mental health nurse and researcher Tony Gillam (2018) found that creative activities can boost your mood and improve your overall psychological well-being. Just as exercise can be used as a preventive aid or to immediately change your moods during difficult times, creativity does the same thing for us. Creative activities include drama, music, writing, dance, photography, knitting, pottery, painting, doodling, drawing, and coloring, among others.

To use creativity as a preventive aid, focus on activities that require repetition, like knitting or coloring, as these can put you in a meditative flow and help quiet the mind. For overall mood management, it also might be beneficial to find activities you can do with groups, like drama or music, as you'll get the added benefit of social connection and belonging. When in need of an immediate mood changer during hard times, focus on creative activities like drawing or painting, as they allow you to express emotions that you may have been suppressing or are unable to articulate with words.

Experiment with creativity and focus on the process, not the result. When using creativity for overall or immediate mood regulation, it's not about the finished product; it's about calming the mind, expressing emotions, and improving your mood. It doesn't matter if your creation ends up in the garbage or a gallery as long as it helps change a negative state of mind into a more positive or productive one.

We're going to combine two of the tools above to give you a whole new self-regulation strategy for dealing with hard feelings. Are you ready? You're going to color to music.

To get set up for this one, find crayons, markers, colored pencils, or paints and paper. Once you have your supplies in front of you, create a fifteen- to twenty-minute playlist, or choose an album that elicits feelings of optimism, relaxation, or calm. If you can, light a candle or burn incense.

Now that you have everything set and ready to go, you're going to draw while listening to your music. You can create outlines of shapes that you color in, create line drawings, or draw a complete picture. There are no rules on what you can or can't draw here. The only rule is that you don't judge your creation and don't focus too much on the result. This exercise is about changing your mood and not about becoming the next Frida Kahlo. You can even destroy it when you're done if you prefer. Just don't stop until your playlist or album is done. Enjoy!

You can combine other self-regulation tools as well to enhance enjoyment and to further engage your brain. Perhaps you draw while in nature or listen to music while exercising. Experiment and try out different combos so you can see what works best for you.

This chapter presented a whole lot of information with some tools for you to practice on your own. We covered what it means to be emotionally dysregulated, how to identify dysregulation when it's happening to you, when to vent and when to shut it down, self-regulation tools, and how to build resilience. That was a lot of work! Go get some fresh air, move your body, and I'll see you when you're ready for the next chapter.

Vibe-Check Your Goals

Remember those goals you set during chapter 4? We're going to revisit them during the rest of the book to help you monitor your progress and stay on track. If you're serious about achieving your goals, then you'll need to be serious about the vibe checks too. People don't just miraculously reach their goals; they set goals that are realistic, authentic, and manageable *and* they work toward them daily. So you've already done the first part during chapter 4, when you set goals that are aligned with your feelings, mapped them out, and scheduled when you'll do the work. Let's check in and see how it's going.

Grab your goal list, calendar, and journal.

- Review your calendar and see what steps you've already achieved toward each of your goals. In your journal, look at the section where you mapped out your goals. Cross off the completed steps and review what still needs to be done.

- Do steps need to be moved to different dates on your calendar? If so, go ahead and do so now.

- How have time-sucks/barriers impacted you from working toward your goals? What changes need to be made? Make notes in your journal about how you will create these changes, and make adjustments on your calendar.

- Did you remember to reward yourself for completing certain steps? If not, make sure you do so now!

CHAPTER 6

Foundational Skill: Awareness of Others

We just came off a pretty big chapter with a ton of information and lots of new skills to practice. Hopefully you took a break before heading right into this new one so that your brain has had a chance to digest and process everything you learned. This chapter will be a bit different from the others because, instead of focusing on internal awareness, we're going to be looking outward. We're going to build awareness of others' emotions, physical states, thoughts, and behaviors. When we know how others might be feeling or thinking, we can better understand their intentions and predict their actions. Understanding others better leads to improved communication and relationships.

You might be thinking, *This doesn't make sense. Self-awareness is about being aware of the self, not other people. Why are we going to try and understand others' emotions, thoughts, and actions? That's on them! It's not my job to know this stuff.* But self-awareness includes understanding how we interact with the world around us and being able to interpret how others feel and think, how they act, and how they perceive us. Take a moment to imagine *not* having this awareness and going through life oblivious to others' emotions and behaviors. You'd be completely unaware of how they might be thinking or what they're thinking about you. You would likely find yourself saying the wrong thing much of the time and then wondering what you possibly could have done wrong. You'd probably even end up in conflicts with friends because you'd misinterpret their actions or things they'd said. When you think of it that way, the necessity of this external awareness makes more sense, doesn't it?

Let's consider it a bit more:

Maddy is in her first year of college and lives in a dorm with a roommate and two suitemates. She just received a D on a huge midterm paper in a class she's barely attended. Tears well up in her eyes, her body tenses, and she walks out of class with fists clenched. Back at her dorm room, she finds a cheerful roommate who's excited that it's Friday and is ready to celebrate a completed lab project that she's been working hard on all semester. Their suitemates are singing along to a favorite song and dancing around the room, grabbing the roommate to celebrate her success. Maddy immediately snaps at her roommate for leaving clothes on the floor and starts complaining about how messy the roommate is. Her roommate stares at the floor, her face gets red, and she starts silently picking her things up. Maddy walks around the room slamming dresser drawers closed, picking up dirty dishes, and yelling about how she can't live like this and maybe she should just drop out and move home. The suitemates quietly back out of the room. Her roommate's mouth drops open and she starts crying. She points out that Maddy has never complained before and that it's not that big a mess. Maddy mumbles that she's just gotten so used to living with a slob that she hasn't said anything until now. The roommate storms off into the suitemates' room and Maddy can hear the three of them leave, letting the door slam behind them.

You know that if Maddy were working on improving her self-awareness, she would've recognized her emotions and thoughts after getting her midterm score back. You also know that if Maddy were working on emotional growth, she would've regulated herself with tools before even coming back to her dorm room. She would've spent time reflecting and learning from the situation so that she could do things differently going forward. But what about awareness of others' emotions? How might that have changed things?

Let's rewrite the story:

Maddy is in her first year of college and lives in a dorm with a roommate and two suitemates. She just received a D on a huge midterm paper in a class she's barely attended. She takes a moment to notice that she feels disappointed in herself for not putting in effort, shame for having blown off so many classes, guilt over the money wasted on this class, sadness in seeing her grade, and anger about the time she wasted doing absolutely nothing instead of going to class. She decides to take a walk to clear her head and focuses on slowing down her breathing while she walks. She starts to feel calmer, so she heads back to her dorm, but before going upstairs, she stops off at the study room to come up with a study plan. She decides how much time she'll spend on the course each week, makes sure she has alerts set on her phone to remind her to attend class and study, and emails her professor to let her know of her plan for accountability. By the time she enters her dorm room, she's feeling more in control of her feelings and her situation. Her roommate announces that she's done with her huge lab project and wants to celebrate the start of the weekend. Their suitemates are singing along to a favorite song and dancing around the room, grabbing the roommate to celebrate her success. Maddy tells her how happy she is that she's done and knows how hard she worked on it. She adds that she wants to celebrate but is still feeling bummed herself. Her roommate is excited and jumping around, so Maddy doesn't elaborate further, as she wants her friend to enjoy the occasion. She suggests that the roommate and suitemates go to lunch first, giving Maddy a little more time to regulate herself alone. Maddy then suggests that they all meet up at their favorite café for dessert at a certain time. Her roommate expresses gratitude and appreciation for the suggestions, and they leave for their celebratory lunch.

Maddy recognized how happy and excited her roommate was and understood that her current mood would negatively affect the entire vibe of the group. She observed the celebratory behaviors of the group and knew that she needed more time to regulate so she could join them in a better mood. She was able to communicate these things in a way that did not ruin her friend's mood or success and also did not make the situation about herself. Her self-awareness helped her identify her own feelings and regulate her emotions and mood. Her awareness of others' emotions and behaviors allowed her to be a good friend and roommate and not spoil someone else's big accomplishment.

How to Understand Others Better

We just saw how an awareness of others' internal states can improve our relationships, decrease conflict, and improve our communication. But being aware of how someone else is feeling or thinking can also lead to a better understanding of their intentions and to the ability to predict their actions. If you're aware that your mom is stressed about a big work project, you're more likely to understand why she's quiet on the drive home from lacrosse practice rather than thinking it means you're in trouble for something. Or if you understand that your friend is worried about her dad's current health issue, you'll probably let it slide when she ignores you in the hall or doesn't respond to texts. And if you know your brother just got in big trouble and is grounded from the homecoming dance, you can likely predict he's not going to want to help you with your homework or play video games later.

When we better understand how others might be feeling or thinking, we're less likely to misinterpret their actions and more likely to know what to expect with how they behave. But how do we do this? How do we figure out what others might be feeling and thinking? It doesn't require any mind-reading skills, but you will need to practice, because just like any other skill, the more you do it, the better you become.

Consider what you know about the person. When we spend a lot of time with others, we tend to learn things about them. Like how you know that one friend gets irritable in crowds while another friend loves the energy of a big group. Or how you know your little sister gets hangry just before dinner and your parents usually fall asleep on the couch by nine. You've been noticing things about the people around you your whole life, and now you get to apply all the bits of observations you've gathered. When you're trying to understand someone better, take a moment to think of these observations and how this information might help you figure them out right now.

Consider the current context or situation. Look at what's going on around the individual and reflect on how this environment might be impacting them. Is noise causing total sensory overload, resulting in someone who can't hear or think clearly? Are they doing something that requires a lot of attention, like driving or trying to figure out a new recipe, so they can't focus as much on you? Also consider what they've shared with you about their current life situation. Perhaps your friend told you how her grandmother is in the hospital or your dad mentioned a difficult client he's been dealing with at work. Think about how this information might be impacting their emotions, thoughts, and behaviors.

Ask questions. It's okay to check in with others and see what they might be thinking and feeling. I mean, you're not actually a mind reader, right? Plus, when you ask how they're feeling or want to hear about their day, it not only gives you context but also allows them to feel heard. So as you're trying to decide if Mom is in the right mood to talk to you about the summer job you want, take a moment first to see how her doctor's appointment went that day and to check in on what kind of mood she's in just then. Or if you're unsure whether your friend is mad at you specifically or the world in general, talk to him about what he did all weekend while his stepbrother was visiting or how he feels about the last-minute announcement of a science test this week.

Give space. Sometimes people aren't in a headspace where they can share what they're feeling or thinking, no matter how great your questions are. And sometimes you can't figure out why they're in the mood they're in, given everything you know about them and their current situation. This is when you might need to take a step back and give them a bit of space. Maybe they're working through something that has nothing to do with you and they need time. Or perhaps they're upset with you specifically but don't know how to bring it up. Giving someone space is a kind and loving way to show respect. It might mean not texting again until they respond to the other texts you already sent, not asking them why they're sitting with someone else at lunch that day, or doing your homework someplace other than the kitchen while your dad makes dinner. Giving space does *not* mean giving someone the cold shoulder and ignoring them. Instead, after you've asked your questions from the previous step, you let them know you're around when they're ready to talk.

Make a private prediction and see if you're right. Doing this requires practice. Part of your practice is to take the information that you know about the person, what you think about their current situation or context, and answers from the questions they gave you to come up with a prediction of what they're thinking and feeling, as well as how you think they'll act. If your dad is driving you to a friend's house after a long day of work, and you know he's been dealing with a difficult client, you might predict that he's stressed out and would rather not talk much but instead would enjoy music. You change the music on your phone to the eighties station, knowing he loves that one best, and then sit back and watch. Does his mood change a bit? Does he seem more relaxed? Or you know that your friend's stepbrother drives him crazy and is always breaking his things, so you predict he'll be in a bad mood after the weekend visit and won't want to go to guitar club on Monday like he normally does. You still ask him to join but don't take it personally when he says no.

Grab your journal and think of an interaction you've had recently that was confusing. Perhaps a friend was aloof or seemed annoyed when you were sharing a story with the group. Or maybe your supervisor at work was more critical than usual of your performance. Or possibly your parent has been irritable lately and snapped at you over a messy room. Got something in mind? Write about the situation in your journal, but instead of writing about it from your perspective, write about it as though you are an observer who watched the situation unfold. Keep your summary of the situation as objective as you can and limit it to three to five sentences. Now we're going to follow the steps from above.

Consider what you know about the person. Write a few things you know about this person that might be relevant to the situation, and include personality traits. For example, the aloof friend isn't a morning person or the grumpy parent has been complaining about a lack of sleep lately.

Consider the current context or situation. Write about the environment in which the confusing interaction took place. From an observer's perspective, what else was going on around you and the other person? Were there other things pulling at their attention or energy? Take a step back and consider the bigger picture. What else could have impacted the situation?

Ask questions. If you could go back in time, what questions would you want to ask the person to gain clarification? How do you think they would have answered? Write the questions and their answers. Is it too late to ask these questions now?

Give space. Write down how much space you think you should give right now. If it's a friend who hasn't been around as much lately, you might try to arrange a get-together in the group chat you're both part of, so it's not a big deal if they don't respond. If it's a family member, you might give them space in the house during downtime but attempt engaging again over your next meal. If it's a supervisor, coworker, teacher, coach, or classmate, you'd likely do better just waiting until you see them again at work, practice, or school.

Make a private prediction and see if you're right. Considering all the information above, write about what you think is going on for them and what you think might have happened during the confusing interaction. Predict what you think will happen next. Don't share the prediction with anyone; just keep it to yourself, wait, and see if you're correct.

Protecting Yourself While Tuning In

For many adolescents, tuning into others' internal states can be a tricky area to navigate. Sometimes you might find yourself swaying too far into the territory of external awareness and focusing so much on how others feel and think that you neglect your own feelings and thoughts. I see this most often in teens and young adults who are crushing on someone, just starting off dating, or falling in love. They get so lost in trying to figure out what the other person is thinking and feeling, so consumed with what they might say or do, that they stop paying attention to their own feelings, thoughts, and behaviors.

Maybe this has happened to you. Perhaps there was a time when you were so excited about your new romance that all you did was try to predict what might be going on inside their head or interpret what they meant with every word. Or maybe you were crushing so hard on the guy who sat next to you in lab that all you could do was wait for his next move. And while you were so busy predicting, interpreting, and waiting, you forgot all about your own feelings and thoughts. So when they were ready to get more serious, it felt shocking to realize that you actually didn't have any shared interests and were kind of bored most of the time hanging out. Or when he finally asked you out, it was suddenly clear that you didn't really like him anymore.

How can we tune into others while maintaining our own self-awareness? The steps below can help you be present with others and notice what's going on with them while not losing yourself in the process.

Ground yourself. Tune into your own feet and notice how they feel, whether that's feeling them touching the ground or noticing them inside your shoes. Try and notice each toe, and see if you can feel the ball and heel of each foot. Put all your focus on your feet until you're aware of where they are in space and how they feel. When we pay attention to our physical bodies, we're establishing a clear boundary between ourselves and others, which is especially helpful when we're around people we want to impress.

Make your breathing slow and steady. We're social creatures, and we subconsciously match our breathing to those around us. And when you like the person near you, you're even more likely to align your breathing with theirs. The problem with this is that breathing patterns can trigger physiological responses. For example, if they're feeling anxious, their breathing is going to be quicker and shallower. You subconsciously match their breathing, and now you're breathing quicker and shallower. And this quicker breathing now causes your heart rate to speed up and tricks your brain into thinking you're feeling anxious. Suddenly you *are* feeling anxious, just like them—and all because of breathing! But you can prevent this from happening by focusing on keeping your own breathing slow and steady no matter how those around you are breathing. This way you won't be susceptible to subconscious matching.

Tell yourself, *Their feelings aren't my feelings.* Make this statement your mantra. Repeat it over and over while you're with them so you don't confuse their feelings for your own. If the guy from lab is acting giggly and interested in you, remind yourself that those are his feelings and not your own. Or if the girl you're starting to date appears disinterested on Facetime, repeat the mantra so you don't confuse her feelings for yours.

Practice creating emotional boundaries with others. You don't need to practice with someone you're into; you can practice this with anyone. Write down the steps of grounding yourself, making your breathing slow and steady, and the mantra of "their feelings aren't my feelings" on your planner, or make it your home screen. The next time you're hanging out with someone, try and notice what they're feeling, thinking, and doing while staying connected to your own body and breath and repeating your new mantra.

After you've practiced, answer these questions in your journal:

- What did you notice about their feelings, thoughts, and actions?

- How did it feel to practice the steps while still being present with them? What was hard about it? What was easy?

- Were you able to not take on their feelings as your own, or did you find that you still did, despite following the steps?

- What do you need to do differently in your next social interaction to follow the steps more easily?

The Social Comparison Trap

This is a big one. The social comparison trap—it's very real, very constant, and very difficult.

Note: *There are multiple forms of comparison, and some are actually helpful! For example, we might push ourselves harder when comparing ourselves to those doing something we desire to do better. Or we might feel better about our situation when we compare ourselves to those in less fortunate circumstances. For this section though, we'll focus solely on social comparison.*

Everyone deals with it, although not everyone will admit that they do, and we all get pulled in at different levels of depth daily. Plus, we're affected differently by it each day, depending on a variety of other factors going on in our lives, like how much sleep we got the night before, whether we're getting along with our friends, how we did on a recent test, whether we made the team, how we're getting along with our parents, and other stuff like that. As an adolescent, you're more susceptible to the social comparison trap because you're in a developmental stage where you feel as though you have an audience most of the time. This imaginary audience won't stay with you forever, but it sure feels real right now.

So just to be clear, the social comparison trap is when we get caught in a trap of comparing ourselves with others and we just can't seem to get out of it. Maybe you get a test back that you earned a B on and you're feeling pretty proud—you studied hard, it was difficult content, and you think a B is pretty good. But then you overhear some other students talking about how bad they did and how they can't believe they got an A- when it was the easiest test in the world. Suddenly, you're feeling bad about your B. Why? Because you've been sucked into the trap. Instead of focusing on how hard you worked to get a grade you were proud of, you're now comparing yourself to your peers and feeling bad about your grade. You think that, because they received better grades and said the test was easy, you should've done better.

Or maybe there's a girl you don't really like—she gossips constantly, is practically a bully to other girls on social media, dresses in a way you would never want to, and doesn't have any of the same interests as you. You're perfectly fine not being friends with her. But one day, your friend group starts to welcome her in, and before you know it, she's sitting with you at lunch and hanging out with all your friends between every single class. Your friends are constantly talking about how funny she is and how cool she dresses, and they love everything she posts on social media. And now you find yourself doubting who you are. You start thinking that your wardrobe is stupid, you don't have enough followers on social media, and your sports and hobbies are dumb. Why the change? You guessed it—you've been pulled into the trap. You're comparing yourself to this other girl, which is making you feel bad about yourself. You think that because your friends are in love with her, there must be something wrong with you.

Here are signs that you've been pulled into the social comparison trap:

You're instantly filled with self-doubt about something you previously felt okay about. You felt great about making the JV team until you heard that the kid who lives down the street from you made varsity. Now you don't even want to play at all and are thinking about quitting the sport you've played for practically your whole life.

You feel bad about your skills or abilities after seeing or hearing about someone you think is better than you. You've been teaching yourself how to play the guitar and are thinking of performing in the upcoming talent show, but you just overheard some of the popular girls talking about the guy they think is so hot who is *unbelievable* on the guitar. You think there's no way you're as good as he is and decide right there on the spot that you'll never play in front of anyone *ever*.

You feel bad about your appearance after seeing or hearing about someone who you think looks better than you. Your older sister went with you to get your hair cut and convinced you to go with a completely different look. You're thinking your new hairdo is pretty cool until you see someone's post on social media of her newly dyed purple-and-blue hair, with a ton of likes and comments about how great she looks. Now you're wishing you could undo your new hairdo and hate your sister for making you do it.

You suddenly feel embarrassed about something that you were previously proud of. Your science olympiad team made the finals, and you were a huge part of the team's success. After a pizza celebration, the team decides to wear their team shirts to school the next day. You show up at school proudly wearing your shirt and instantly hear a group of kids laughing at the "nerds" in their "loser science shirts." You go into the bathroom to turn yours inside out before anyone can see it.

You catch yourself saying negative things to yourself when around certain people. You're really excited about having new friends and a huge group to sit with at lunch now, but you notice that whenever you're with them, you're telling yourself to shut up or that what you just said was dumb.

How do you avoid the trap? And how do you pull yourself out once you've realized that you've been sucked in? Here are some strategies to help:

First and foremost, practice good self-care daily. Remember the mental vaccine from chapter 4? When you exercise good self-care habits like eating healthy, getting enough sleep each night, and getting some exercise each day, you're more likely to be able to handle tough things. If you're not getting enough sleep and surviving on junk food, you're starting at a deficit each day and will be more likely to get pulled into the trap.

Pay attention to when you're more prone to falling into the trap. Do you find that you're more likely to fall into it when around certain people? Or is it when you're on social media? Practice paying attention to when you feel it and make a mental note of "Hey, I'm feeling pretty crappy about myself right now," so you can see if any patterns emerge.

Stay away from the stuff that makes you feel like crap. If you've been paying attention to when you're more likely to fall into the trap and noticed that you always fall into it when looking at a particular person's social media account or when hanging out with a specific friend, maybe it's time for a break. Unfollow the account or take some time away from the friend and see how you feel then. Maybe it's something they're doing that's making you feel bad or perhaps it's your own low self-esteem. Either way, a break will help you decide.

Remember that there's no right or wrong way to look, think, or live in the world. When you're in the trap, use self-talk to try and get out of it. Tell yourself that everyone has different skills, abilities, qualities, personality traits, looks, strengths, and weaknesses, and that this is what makes us all unique. How boring would life be if we were all the same?

Keep in mind that life isn't a contest. Everyone develops at different rates. A certain skill or ability may really click with a peer now and may click with you next year. Or you may be good at one thing this year and a friend may learn how to do it in college. We all develop differently and at our own speeds.

Practice gratitude. Instead of feeling left out when you see friends together online, practice being grateful for what you're doing in that moment. Instead of comparing your grade to someone else's, try focusing on how hard you worked to get yours and how proud you are for putting in the effort.

Work on building your own self-confidence. Focus on the things you like about yourself, the stuff you're good at, and the things that go right each day. Keep track of your strengths and passions while paying special attention to the things that are working out for you.

Consider the signs of being pulled into the social comparison trap. Go back and review them and grab your journal. Reflect on and answer these questions:

- Which signs have you noticed in yourself?

- Which signs show up for you the most? Why do you think that is?

Next consider the strategies list. Review it and notice which ones you've tried on your own. Reflect on and answer these questions:

- Which strategies have you used before? How did they work for you? What would you do differently next time to ensure that they work differently?

- Which strategies have you not tried yet? When do you think they'll be useful? How can you ensure that you'll remember to use them when needed?

Now that we spent a chapter looking outward, we're going to turn back inward for the next chapter and consider physical sensations. The next chapter will also be our final foundational skills chapter! You've been working so hard building your self-awareness and practicing self-regulation, I really hope you're proud of yourself. Take a moment and consider your progress. So often we're focused on looking forward that we forget to notice our gains. Think of where you were at the start of this book and all that you've learned. Take time to reflect on your growth before moving on to the next chapter. Once you've done that, I'll see you there.

Vibe-Check Your Goals

Grab your journal and look at your goal list. Considering each of your goals, reflect on and answer these questions:

- What have I been doing to work toward my goals?

- How do I feel about my progress so far?

- What do I need to do to stay on track?

Using the feeling wheel from chapter 2, examine how you feel about each goal currently. Take a moment to look at your most important goal. Imagine that you've achieved it. Really try and put yourself in that version of yourself, the version that is now living with the results of having achieved the goal. Which feeling from the wheel does that spark? Write that feeling next to the first ranked goal.

Now move down your goal list, imagining that you've achieved each one, one at a time. Write the feeling from the wheel that is sparked by having met each goal. Considering the sparked feelings from this visualization exercise, are there any goals that need to be eliminated? Do any of the goals need to be moved up or down on your list?

Make any necessary changes to your goal list.

CHAPTER 7

Foundational Skill: Understanding Physical Sensations

Welcome to the last foundational skill! You've covered some serious ground, my friend. You've built your awareness of feelings, thoughts, and behaviors. You've set goals that are aligned with your true self and are working toward achieving them. You've become more aware of others and how you impact them and they you. And you've learned so many self-regulation skills and tools that you're ready for anything!

For our final skill, we're going back to our bodies to better understand physical sensations so you can connect them appropriately with emotions; however, we're going to make sure that you don't become *overly* sensitive to these sensations. I'm also going to teach you one of my favorite tricks—turning anxiety into excitement. And we're going to cover low motivation since this often shows up in the body through fatigue, apathy, and lethargy. We'll discuss some ways to break the low-motivation cycle when you feel like you just can't get out of it.

You might be wondering, *Why save this for the final skill? This seems pretty important; shouldn't we have covered it earlier?* While it's incredibly important to be able to tune into our physical sensations and connect them with our emotions, I've found that it's also incredibly difficult for many to do. After working with adolescents for so long, I've realized that when we build self-awareness in all the other areas first, it's much easier to recognize the connections with physical sensations later. We're going to do things a bit differently this time around though. We're going to start with an exercise to set the mood. So find a private space, kick off your shoes, and get ready to tune into your body.

We're going to do a body scan. First, you'll read through the directions fully so you know what to do, and then you'll close your eyes and go through them from memory. If you need to record the directions and listen to them instead, go right ahead. Or if you need to sneak a peek at the steps as you do them from memory, that's fine too. This isn't about perfection and memorization; this is about tuning into body sensations.

- Starting with your feet, focus on how they feel. Wiggle your toes and notice any sensations. Pay attention to temperature (are they hot, warm, cold?) and texture (can you feel the cotton of your socks or the hardwood floors?). Now try and feel your feet without moving a single muscle. What do you notice when you do that?

- Move up to your calves and do the same thing. Notice how they feel, flex your muscles, and pay attention to any sensations. Is there a temperature you can feel? What about texture? Now try and feel your calves without moving a muscle and see what you notice.

- Keep moving up your body, focusing on one muscle group at a time. From your calves, go to your thighs, then to your glutes. You can then move to your abs, lower back, upper back, and chest. From there, jump down to your hands and then move up your arms to your forearms, biceps, triceps, and shoulders. Finish with your neck, face, and head. With each muscle group, focus on observing sensations, temperature, and textures. Wiggle or flex the muscles and see what you notice. Also be sure to notice how that muscle group feels without flexing or moving a thing.

The order of moving around your body isn't important, so if you do it differently, that's fine. The order isn't the point. The point of this exercise is to learn how to tune into how your body feels. You'll likely find that you notice sensations in some body parts easily and that you have difficulty noticing in other areas. That's normal!

Check in with yourself once you're done by pulling out your journal and completing these prompts and questions:

It was difficult for me to _____. Why was this challenging? Is there anything I can do to make it easier in the future?

It was easy for me to _____. Why was this so easy for me?

What did I learn from this exercise?

When would be a good time to do body scans in my daily life?

Connecting Mind and Body

Now that you've completed a body scan, let's consider what sensations can mean. Sometimes our sensations are connected to our thoughts and feelings. These sensations provide us with information on how we're thinking or feeling. They might support what we already know or help us make sense of it all. They can be the key indicator telling us how we're feeling or thinking, or they might just point us in the right direction. But not all sensations mean something and not all sensations are connected to our emotions. We'll dive into that in the next section. For now, we'll examine the ones that do mean something—the physical sensations that are connected to our emotions and thoughts.

In one study, researchers found that the basic emotions (anger, fear, happiness, disgust, sadness, surprise, and neutrality) were all felt in the chest region, like heart rate and changes in breathing. But more specifically, anger was also felt in the upper arms, sadness was felt through a decrease in arm and leg sensations, disgust was felt in the digestive system and throat, and happiness was felt through an increase in sensations throughout the entire body (Nummenmaa et al. 2013). The same researchers did another study in 2018 and found that the stronger you feel an emotion in your body, the stronger it becomes in your mind (Nummenmaa et al. 2018).

Perhaps you can relate to this finding by recalling a time when you felt all kinds of physical sensations before giving a presentation in class, which in turn increased your anxiety. Let's pretend you were slightly nervous heading into the classroom, knowing you were going first. But then your stomach started to churn, you suddenly felt hot and flushed, and there was a lump in your throat that seemed to come out of nowhere. Because these physical sensations were so strong, you decided you must be extremely anxious (even though you were only slightly nervous initially).

One book about treating emotional disorders emphasized the need to focus on what the physical sensations mean to the individual instead (Barlow et al. 2017). For example, if you're about to walk into a job interview and feel butterflies in your stomach, how you interpret those butterflies will affect your behavior. If you view butterflies as a sign that you're getting really nervous, you'll likely trigger more sensations like getting hot and sweaty, shaking knees, and a trembling voice. Your thoughts might even become more negative. However, if you interpret the butterflies as a normal reaction that sometimes occurs in high-pressure situations, you won't focus on them and will walk into your interview ready to go and in a better mindset.

An older but still relevant model breaks emotions up by high and low energy. In this model, high-energy positive emotions include excitement, delight, and astonishment. Low-energy positive emotions include pleasure, contentment, relaxation, and calmness. In contrast, high-energy negative emotions include anger, fear, and alarm, while low-energy negative emotions include depression, boredom, and tiredness (Russell 1980). Even though this model doesn't specify physical sensations, it can be helpful to consider your own energy level when trying to understand what you're feeling.

Let's break down what high and low energy means. High energy is when we want to move our bodies; low energy is when we don't. Suppose your body feels jittery, fidgety, and on edge, which are all high-energy feelings. According to Russell's model, that might mean you're feeling excitement, delight, astonishment, anger, fear, or alarm. But because you also looked at the context and considered that you were checking your email for a college acceptance, you determine that you're excited. In contrast, suppose you're feeling like you can't get off the couch and your body feels heavy, like the very idea of getting up and doing something sounds like too much. These low-energy feelings might mean you're feeling pleasure, contentment, relaxation, calmness, depression, boredom, or tiredness. If you also considered the context of how you've been scrolling mindlessly on your phone for a long time and know from experience that this activity sucks your energy, you'd be able to determine that you're bored.

On the flip side, sometimes our emotions, thoughts, and environment impact our physical selves and we experience sensations as a direct result of one or more of those things (Yarwood 2022). Perhaps you're falling in love and whenever you see your new love, your entire body instantly feels light and tingly. Or you're thinking all kinds of worry thoughts about an upcoming project, and soon you notice tension in your shoulders and an upset stomach. Maybe you're walking into the concert venue of your favorite musician who you've been waiting to see for months, and you notice that your heart is racing, your knees are trembling, and you feel hot. None of those physical sensations were present prior to seeing your love, thinking worry thoughts, or entering the concert venue. Those feelings, thoughts, and the environment created them.

Physical sensations are one piece of understanding yourself better, but they aren't the sole component. Think of them as data points. You're collecting data that will all be put together to create one whole picture. Other data points include the situation or context, like you saw above. Another data point to consider is your thoughts. You've worked on self-awareness of thoughts and have the skills to recognize your self-talk and when it's impacting your feelings and behaviors. When you consider all the data, you'll likely be able to better understand your physical sensations and yourself.

What does it look like when you put it all together? Grab your journal to make any notes of what you notice or any thoughts that pop into mind as you're doing this.

- Do a quick body scan to notice where in your body you're experiencing physical sensations.

- Pay attention to the strong sensations. For example, if you were to rate each sensation on a scale of 1–10, with 1 meaning you barely notice it and 10 meaning you can't stop thinking about it, home in on the ones you rate at a 7 and above. Let go of ones that are a 6 and below.

- Considering sensations that are a 7 and above, what emotions could they be connected to based on their location in your body? Are they high- or low-energy sensations? What do these sensations mean to you?

- Think about your current situation and context. What clues can you find that might help you connect the physical sensations with your emotions? Could your current situation be impacting how your body feels? Or could your physical sensations be changing how you're interpreting your current situation?

- Notice your thoughts. Do a brain dump if needed. (Remember this one? We covered it in chapter 1.) What thoughts are circulating in your head? Are they positive, negative, neutral? How might they be contributing to your physical sensations? How might your physical sensations be changing your thoughts?

- When you consider everything from above, how does it all fit together? What is your body trying to tell you? How are your current thoughts, feelings, and situation impacting how your body feels?

Avoiding Overthinking Physical Sensations

Sometimes people become overly sensitive to body sensations and interpret every single one as meaning something, when that's just not the case. Not every physical sensation is linked with our minds. Our bodies are constantly working, and sometimes that work can create sensations. And these sensations have absolutely nothing to do with our emotions, thoughts, or situations. You might be wondering what the harm is in being tuned into every sensation you experience. The answer is that when we're so focused on our inner world, whether it's physical sensations, feelings, or thoughts, we're missing out on our external world. We're missing out on experiences and relationships; we're missing out on participating in life.

How do you know if this is you? How do you know if you're overly focused on physical sensations? Consider these questions:

- Do you find yourself constantly aware of what you're feeling physically?

- Do you experience a lot of minor or vague health issues like mild stomachaches or headaches, body aches, or muscle pains?

- Do people point out to you that you complain about body aches and pains a lot?

- Do you find that you miss out on things because of undiagnosed physical complaints?

If you found yourself answering yes to many of the above questions, the good news is that you're super in tune with your body. You feel physical sensations easily and that's great! The not-so-great news is that you might be giving too much weight to these physical sensations and allowing them to have too much power over you. Remember when I mentioned earlier how we want to use physical sensations as data points? Well, you might be using them as the complete picture, rather than just one point that makes up the picture. You want to give the physical sensations the same value as other data points such as your feelings, thoughts, and the context. You don't want to give your physical sensations more value than any other data point.

Earlier you read that how people think about their physical sensations can determine their emotional experience. If you're someone who notices everything going on inside, you might find that your emotions are harder to tolerate. Let's consider this for a moment. Suppose that you notice fatigue, low energy, and a headache as you're getting ready for the day. You interpret these physical feelings as meaning you're depressed. Now you start thinking negative thoughts like, *Today's going to be so hard,* and *I have no motivation and so much to do.* Your depression now feels even heavier and harder to manage, so you decide to call in sick to work and get back into bed. Your physical sensations determined how you felt and, because you focused so much on these sensations, your emotions felt too hard to manage.

It can be tricky to know when to pay attention to physical sensations and when to dismiss them, but just like everything else, it's a learning process. As you learn how to tune into your body, practice letting go of the sensations that don't provide much value. Recall the previous exercise where you rated sensations and had to let go of any that were a 6 or below. Make that your practice so you're not focusing on the smaller ones. And if you can't recall how to let go, go back to chapter 5 to review and practice. If you find that you rate every physical sensation high and that most sensations are difficult for you to tolerate, start with the one that is most tolerable. Practice letting that one go so you can still participate in things, and continue practicing until it's no longer preventing you from doing the things you're scheduled to do. Once you notice progress, move on to the next sensation that's most tolerable and do the same thing. Be patient with yourself as you go and know that it'll get better with time.

One of my favorite tricks to play on my brain is to turn anxiety into excitement. It's easier and simpler than it sounds. In fact, you might read the description below and think it won't work, but I assure you, it does! According to Russell's model, excitement and fear are both high-energy emotions (1980). Anxiety falls under the umbrella of fear, so we can deduce that anxiety is also a high-energy emotion. Consider the physical sensations you experience when you're excited. Most of us would likely list a racing heart, jitteriness, and fidgeting. Would you add anything else? Maybe a bit of a churning stomach? Now consider the physical sensations that you experience when you're anxious. You'd likely say racing heart, jitteriness, fidgeting, and a churning stomach. Look familiar? The sensations for both feelings are pretty similar for most of us, so we can use that to our own benefit.

The next time you notice the physical sensations above, instantly tell yourself, *I'm so excited about* (whatever the current situation or context is that's creating the sensations)! Don't allow your brain to even consider anxiety as an option—just focus on being excited!

Next, focus on all the things that you're excited about with the situation. What are you looking forward to? What's good about the situation? What could go right and work out in your favor with it?

That's it. That's all you do. Don't overcomplicate it. Here's how it might look. You're on your way to your first meeting with an art club where you likely won't know anyone. As you're entering the building, you notice your racing heart and churning stomach. You feel jittery and jumpy inside. You instantly tell yourself, *I'm so excited about this new club! I'll get to use pottery wheels and oil paints, and I'll even try screen printing! I bet I'll learn new art forms and meet some cool artists who like the same things I do!*

Try it out the next time you're experiencing physical sensations of anxiety. Turn it into excitement and see how it changes the course for you.

Dealing with Low Motivation

Low motivation is when you don't have the willingness or desire to do something. It shows up in the body through fatigue, apathy, and lethargy. We're more susceptible to low motivation when dealing with a physical illness, like a cold or flu, since we've likely been recovering in bed or on the couch, watching show after show, and moving very little. We're also more susceptible to low motivation when feeling depressed, bored, or tired (remember the low-energy negative emotions from earlier?). But low motivation can also strike if we're overwhelmed or confused and don't know where to start, or if we're easily distracted and find ourselves going from one shiny object to the next. Whatever the reason, it can be hard to get our bodies and minds willing to do something.

Breaking the cycle of low motivation starts with one step and then continues one single step at a time. And that initial one step is to *do*. It's not to think about doing or to plan out how to do. It's to actually get up and *do*. And then once that first step is done, to move to the next step of doing. And then to the next and the next, doing each step along the way.

My clients with low motivation often want a magic solution that doesn't involve leaving the couch or bedroom. They want a solution where they're miraculously energized and invigorated to get up and do, but I'll tell you the same thing I tell them: motivation comes from doing, not from thinking about doing.

It's frustrating, I know. The last thing you want to do when you're lacking motivation is to have to do something! It doesn't make sense either. I mean, how are you supposed to get motivated by doing something when the whole problem is that you don't have any motivation to do anything? But that's the reality. Motivation comes from doing. It comes from action, not inaction. Now that doesn't mean the action has to be huge or mind-blowing; it can be super small and super simple. It can be taking a shower, going outside, opening a book, turning off the TV, setting up your study area, calling a friend, making a cup of coffee, putting on your workout clothes, or looking up your research topic. Just taking that first single step. And then once you've taken that first one, you focus on the next small step and do it. And then the next small step. And the next. And you keep going until you've completed the task, one small step at a time.

Beware though! While you're completing one step at a time, your brain might try and talk you out of it. You might hear some negative thoughts about how hard it is, how the task isn't really that important, or how one more episode won't hurt. You're going to have to ignore those negative thoughts for now. Don't bother trying to turn them into helpful thoughts; you need to save your energy for doing. Just dismiss them or visualize them going into your brain's garbage bin. Focusing too much on them will only hold you back from the doing.

Another barrier you might encounter is creating steps that are too big or too overwhelming, which will put you right back on the couch. If you're trying to find motivation to write a term paper, and your small step is to create an outline but you haven't even figured out your topic, of course you won't start! That's really overwhelming. Who can create an outline when they don't even know what they're writing about yet? These steps are there to set you up for success, not failure. So if your steps aren't getting you moving, they're too big. Make sure your steps are *small*. And when I say small, think baby steps. Think, *What's the absolute smallest thing I can do right now that will move me in the direction of task completion?* No step is too small!

Think of a chore or task that you must do regularly but suffer from low motivation when it comes time to do it. Maybe it's laundry or meal prep. Perhaps it's the weekly journal entry you must write for your economics class. Or maybe it's the daily exercise you know you're supposed to be doing to improve your mental and physical health. Grab your journal and complete these steps:

- Identify the task of low motivation and write it down.

- Set your timer to three minutes and brainstorm all the possible steps that go into completing this task. You're not worrying about how big or small or even thinking about the order of steps. All you're doing is brainstorming right now. Go until the timer goes off.

- Use another sheet of paper to organize your brainstorming list. Are there any steps that seem too big and overwhelming? Break those down into smaller steps.

- Put your steps in order from the first one you'd need to do to the very last one.

Now you have a plan. When it's time for you to do this task, you'll know exactly which steps to take and in which order. All you have to do is follow your list. Put it where you'll see it when it's time to do the task.

All right, you made it to the end! You now have a better understanding of your physical sensations and what they mean. You also learned how not to overly focus on them so they consume you. You learned how to turn anxiety into excitement and how to deal with low motivation. You've got some good skills, my friend. Ready for the very last chapter? We're going to bring everything together and wrap things up. I'll see you there after the next vibe check.

Vibe-Check Your Goals

Grab your journal and look at your goal list. Considering each of your goals, reflect on and answer these questions:

- Where am I now with meeting my goals?

- How have I been avoiding my goals?

- What's getting in my way?

- What's holding me back?

- What are my current time-sucks, and how can I decrease time spent on them?

- How can I maintain progress?

- What can I do to get back on track?

- What changes do I need to make?

- What's been difficult for me?

CHAPTER 8

Evolving and Growing

Wow, this has been an incredible journey! You've taken time to learn, grow, and develop. You committed yourself to this book and you did the work. Congratulations! I hope you're proud of yourself. Even though I might not know you personally, I'm proud of you. I know how many other things you have tugging at your attention, how many distractions are out there, and how easy it is to convince ourselves that hard work is a waste of time. And yet you persisted. You stayed with it despite all of that. You know what that tells me? I now know that you can accomplish anything you set your mind to. You can achieve your goals. And you're going to do big things with your life. I'm so glad you made this book a part of your journey in doing that. I hope that you reach out to me at https://www.destinationyou.net/connect and share what you're doing. I'd love to follow along.

But I don't want to mislead you. I don't want you to think that it's all roses and sunshine going forward. There's still work to be done, growth to be had, and development to encounter. Emotional intelligence isn't a skill you master and then you're done. It's something that you will be constantly working on for the rest of your life (hopefully!). While you've learned a lot by reading this book and doing the exercises, you're still going to be challenged. You'll find yourself in situations where you're unsure of how you feel or what you're thinking. There are going to be times when you don't know how to regulate your emotions and you feel out of control. And sometimes you might find yourself unsure of how to identify and reach goals that are truly meaningful to you. Each of these things are to be expected. They're normal. They're going to happen. Don't think that because of them, you're failing or doing something wrong.

We'll spend this final chapter on navigating uncertainty of feelings and thoughts, what to do when your emotions feel out of control, and how to get back in touch with your values so that your goals are meaningful to you. But before we do that, let's look at a tool you'll want to become very familiar with as it'll help with uncertainty and out-of-control emotions: self-compassion. We exhibit self-compassion when we take a noncritical stance toward our own inadequacies or failures. Put another way, it's when we view our upsets from a neutral or positive perspective. We don't criticize or look at ourselves negatively; instead, we're kind or understanding. You'll get a chance to practice self-compassion in just a moment, but first, let's see what it looks like in action.

Audrey is a high schooler who's been working hard on her emotional intelligence. She's more self-aware than she was a year earlier and is getting better and better each day at regulating her emotions. She's also focused a lot of effort on her goals, from creating meaningful ones to mapping out each step she needs to take. When she finds herself unable to decide on which college to attend, she feels surprised by her uncertainty. She thinks, *This is what I've been working on all year with my goals! Getting into my dream college! Why do I now feel so unsure if this is the right fit for me?* Because Audrey has recently learned about self-compassion, she quickly recognizes that her thoughts aren't very compassionate toward herself and, in fact, are making her feel worse. She asks herself what she would say to her best friend if she were in the same situation. She changes her thoughts to: *It's okay to feel this way right now. I have time to figure things out. Whatever choice I make will be the right one for now.* This perspective shift allows her to view the situation with a bit more kindness. Now that she feels calmer, she decides to set up meetings with her high school counselor and her diving coach to go over her options and to hear their perspectives. She immediately emails them from her phone and tells herself it's time to focus on something completely different. She grabs her dog's leash and calls for him to go on a walk. She knows that his excitement and walk through the nearby park will stop her from thinking about college and will put her in the present moment.

Audrey could have easily become so frustrated with her indecision that she worked herself up into a state of complete upset. She could have focused on her uncertainty and made it mean something negative about her college goals. She also could have become so down on herself that she was unable to see any options, to take a step back, or to problem solve. Instead, she practiced self-compassion and viewed the situation from a calmer perspective. This allowed her to see that there are people who can guide her through this decision. Once she remembered she had options, she was able to move on to something else.

This exercise is based on the work of Dr. Kristin Neff (2023), a lead researcher on self-compassion.

Notice your self-criticism. As you've been paying attention to your thoughts, you've likely noticed just how cruel you can be to yourself. You've likely found yourself saying things about yourself that you would never say about anyone else. To practice self-compassion, you're going to need to continue to notice these types of thoughts. If we don't notice them, we can't change them.

Change the self-critical thoughts. Now that you're bringing more aware-ness to the self-critical thoughts, you're going to need to change them. And just like with changing any thought, you need to change it to something more useful. It doesn't need to be overly positive (unless you truly believe it), it just needs to be a less critical and more understanding version of the original thought.

Ask yourself what you would you say to a friend in your situation. If you're having trouble coming up with less critical thoughts, imagine that your friend is in your situation. What would you say to that friend? What types of kind, supportive, and useful comments would you make to help them through it? Now apply these thoughts to yourself.

Navigating Uncertainty

You're going to find that there are times when you just can't figure out what you're feeling or thinking. This is to be expected. Sometimes a bunch of feelings and thoughts get muddled together in our heads and, no matter how hard we try, we can't pull them apart. We're unsure of what to do next since we don't even know what we want in the first place. This is going to happen, and in fact, you should expect it! Being uncertain doesn't mean you've "failed" or that you haven't learned anything from this book. It just means that you're human—congratulations!

When navigating uncertainty, start off with self-compassion. Mentally and emotionally beating yourself up isn't going to make things any better for you—it'll actually make things worse—so remind yourself that this is normal and that, while frustrating to go through, eventually, things will become clearer. You can use the self-compassion exercise above to be less self-critical and to talk to yourself the way you would to a friend. Focus on supportive, helpful, and kind thoughts like *I'll get through this,* or *It's okay that I'm feeling this way right now,* or *I'm not supposed to know everything* all *the time.* These types of thoughts are not only self-compassionate, they're also true! Write them down if you need to so they're available when those feelings of uncertainty creep in and take over.

Once you've been a compassionate friend to yourself, take some time away from the situation. Stepping away and focusing on things other than the situation will give your brain a chance to reset. It may sound odd, but our brains do quite a bit of "behind the scenes" work without us even realizing it. Perhaps you can think of a time when you were stuck on a problem or situation, threw up your hands in uncertainty, and went off to do something else. Maybe you went to bed for the night or hung out with friends. But whatever you were doing, you weren't focused on your problem or situation for the time being. And then later when you went back to it, you clearly saw the correct path right in front of you. Everything made sense. It made such sense that you actually wondered how you might have missed it in the first place. That's because while you were busy sleeping or hanging with friends, your brain was doing some serious editing and connecting. And all that editing and connecting allowed for the problem to be solved and for the uncertainty to be cleared up.

But maybe your brain couldn't solve the uncertainty or problem when you stepped away. Perhaps your issue remains, even after the self-compassion and the reset. It's time to grab your journal and do a brain dump. If you don't remember how to do a brain dump, revisit chapter 1 for a review. Brain dumps are helpful when you need to get all your different thoughts and feelings out. Just remember, the purpose isn't to write a college essay, so don't worry about grammar, punctuation, or spelling. You're dumping the contents of your brain out onto your paper without any editing, so it might look ugly. That's fine. The purpose of doing a brain dump here is to give yourself a chance to sort through what you're thinking and feeling without interruption or judgment. You might be surprised by what comes out.

Finally, if the self-compassion, reset, and brain dump don't bring you clarity, it's time to get comfortable with the feeling of uncertainty. Sometimes our thoughts, feelings, or issues can't be sorted out right away. They might take time and numerous bouts of self-compassion, lots of resets, and daily brain dumps. While you're taking the time needed, allow yourself to feel the uncertainty, to notice where in your body you feel it, and to just let it be. Think of it as a houseguest who has decided to extend their visit. A person you must learn to tolerate since they're in your bathroom using your toothpaste, sitting down to dinner with you, and asking to change the channel when you're watching a favorite show. You might want to explode, but realize, it'll be easier to just let them do their thing while you continue to do yours.

Out-of-Control Emotions

Emotional intelligence includes awareness of emotions and self-regulation of big feelings; however, you're likely still going to have times where you feel completely out of control. When your feelings seem so huge that you don't know if you'll ever recover. You might find yourself in a very dysregulated state where you can't stop the crying, yelling, throwing, or whatever it is you're doing while experiencing the massive feelings. You're okay. You're not broken, and this doesn't mean there's no hope for you. It just means that this is an area for growth. If you find yourself in an out-of-control emotional state, do the following:

> **Slow down your breathing.** Our breathing is the first thing to speed up when we're in distress and can trigger other things to start happening in our bodies, like getting hot and sweaty, and feeling like we need to run, fight, or avoid. Stop the process by getting control over your breathing. Just focus on slowing it down, counting while you inhale and exhale, trying to make each breath just a little bit longer until your breathing feels normal for you.

> **Focus on your senses.** Put all your attention and awareness on what you can hear, see, touch, smell, and taste. Get specific and identify things. My favorite way to do this is to name five things I can hear, four things I can

see, three things I can touch, two things I can smell, and one thing I can taste.

Repeat a calming mantra. A mantra is a quick and easy statement we can say to ourselves that will create feelings of peace and calm. It's helpful if you create one ahead of time that you can use during times of distress. I have clients who write their mantras down on sticky notes and leave them in places where they think they might need them. But if you're creating yours during the stressful time, just make it short and believable. Something like *I will survive this*, or *I've been through hard things before, I can get through hard things now*.

And remember, the more you practice these steps when your emotions are high but not yet out of control, the easier it'll be to do it when they are. If you find that you're constantly struggling with out-of-control emotions, there's a good chance that you need to practice these steps more.

Meaningful Goals

Let's talk about how to stay on top of your goals so that you're continuing to work toward things that align with your values. Meaningful goals are ones that match a future for yourself or your life that you're excited about. They're the goals you stick with, even when doing that gets hard and boring, because you know where they'll get you. Meaningful goals are the ones you've created and are motivated to achieve.

Just because a goal is meaningful, though, doesn't mean you're going to wake up every morning jumping out of bed with enthusiasm and excitement to get to work. There are going to be lots of days where it feels monotonous and redundant, where you struggle to do the bare minimum. Think of a swimmer training for the Olympics. Do you think they love getting up super early in the morning every single day? Or that they're motivated to swim lap after lap, hours on end? Absolutely not. They get bored with the constant training, sick of waking up early, and annoyed with doing the same thing day after day.

Overall, meaningful goals will excite you—the big-picture part of the goal is usually what motivates you to keep going. It's the breakdown of the goal, the day-to-day work you must do in order to eventually achieve the big picture, that can get redundant and boring. The swimmer is probably highly motivated by the goal of making it to the Olympics and likely daydreams about that achievement constantly. In fact, that's probably what keeps them going when they're going to bed at 8:00 p.m. to be up by 4:00 a.m. the next day. It's what drives them to work on their stroke and flip turn, what pushes them to perfect their start off the block, and what keeps them showing up each day, practicing the same things over and over. They know that these small things add up over time and will help them reach their bigger goal.

What does this mean for you? You'll want to frequently check in on your goals, like you've been doing in the vibe checks and will do again in a bit with a goal reflection. This checking-in process will ensure that you're working toward something with purpose. You'll also need to use your emotional self-awareness skills and assess how you feel about your goals. Your emotional self-awareness will be your guide to ensuring that your big goals are things you truly want to be doing. Your road map is full of the smaller day-to-day stuff, and while those things might not light you up, if you know they're aligned with your bigger goals, you'll be able to push through.

Finding a Therapist or Coach

Perhaps all this personal growth and discovery has you craving more. Or maybe as you've been working on things, you've realized that there are some areas where you need further help. If so, you might want to consider working individually with a therapist or a coach. A therapist or coach can help you build upon the skills you've started here, teach you new strategies, and help you further your personal growth in a variety of ways. Let's talk about the difference between therapy and coaching and then some ways to find one that's a good fit for you.

The American Psychological Association (APA) defines therapy as "any psychological service provided by a trained professional that primarily uses forms of communication and interaction to assess, diagnose, and treat dysfunctional emotional reactions, ways of thinking, and behavior patterns" (A *Dictionary of Psychology*, 3rd ed., s.v. "therapy"). There are various forms of therapy, and some therapists specialize in a particular area. For example, one therapist might specialize in helping adolescents with anxiety, while another might work only with college students with a diagnosis of attention-deficit/hyperactivity disorder (ADHD). A simple search and a little research will let you know what a therapist specializes in so you can tell if they're right for you.

The APA defines coaching as "specialized instruction and training provided to enable individuals to acquire or enhance particular skills, as in executive coaching or life coaching, or to improve performance, as in athletic or academic coaching" (A *Dictionary of Psychology*, 3rd ed., s.v. "coaching"). Coaches aren't focused so much on dysfunctional emotional reactions, thought patterns, or behaviors; instead, they focus on building upon strengths you already have. They also might help with goal setting and achievement. Like therapists, coaches usually have different areas of specialty. One coach might specialize in helping high school athletes perform better and attain college scholarships, while another might focus on helping young adults transition from living with their parents to living independently.

If you're unsure if a therapist or a coach is the right fit for you, do some further exploration. Most therapists and coaches provide free consultations where you can chat on the phone or do a video call. Some will want your parents present and others may not. They'll ask you questions about what you want to work on and a bit about your history, explain what they do, and discuss how you might work together. You don't have to decide right there on the call; you can take some time to think it through. You can even set up several free consultations and meet with different therapists and coaches until you've found the right fit for you.

Vibe-Check Your Goals

You made it! You made it through the book *and* you made it through your goals. Well, maybe you didn't quite make it through your goal list, so let's see if we can figure out why... Grab your goal list and reflect on and answer these questions:

- Did you put in the work on setting and achieving goals or did you blow it off?

- What would you do differently in the future?

- Which goals did you complete, which ones did you change, and which ones did you not complete?

- Did you create goals that were too big or too small?

- Were your goals aligned with your feelings and values or were they what you thought others wanted you to achieve?

- Were you successful in avoiding the activities or people that hold you back?

- What held you back and why?

- How do you feel about where you are now with each goal?

Just because you're done with the book doesn't mean you have to be done with your goal setting and achievement. You can revisit the goal-setting section, vibe checks, and goal reflection as often as you'd like to work on new goals. You may have even found that you now have a better understanding of goal setting and achievement so you want to start from scratch. Or perhaps you reached many of your goals during this book, so you're ready for fresh ones. Our goals shift and change over time as we reach them and as we change. Just use the tools from this book to help you create ones that are aligned with your true feelings and follow the vibe checks to stay on track and you'll do great.

You've got big things ahead of you in this lifetime. I can't wait to see what you achieve.

This Isn't Good-Bye

Even though we've come to the end of our time together, this isn't good-bye. You're going to continue working on these skills for a long time (as am I!), and our paths might cross again. We might run into each other on social media, in another book, or you might even decide to reach out to me at https://www. destinationyou.net/connect.

Whether we meet again or not, please know that I'm always rooting for you. I'll be over here in my little corner of the world, cheering you on and knowing all that you're capable of.

You've got this.

Feeling Wheel

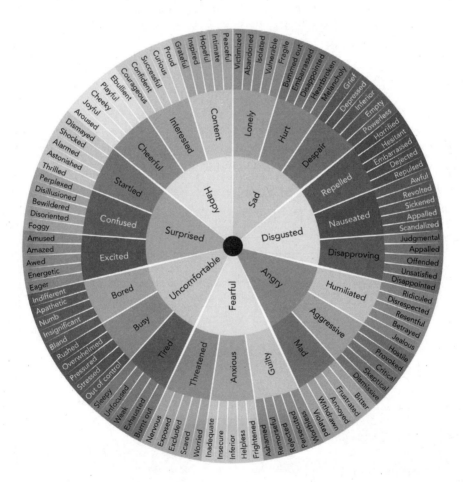

Acknowledgments

With thanks to Jennye Garibaldi for supporting me every step of the way, from conceptualization to development to fine-tuning;

Caleb Beckwith for incredible editorial review and notes;

Callie Brown for thoughtful editorial support;

Karen Schader for making copyediting easy;

Amy Jo Martin for always believing in me, even when I don't believe in myself;

My Renegade crew, who inspire me daily to think and dream big;

and

My teen clients for constantly challenging me to learn and grow so that I can better help you.

References

Armstrong, A. R., R. F. Galligan, and C. Critchley. 2011. "Emotional Intelligence and Psychological Resilience to Negative Life Events." *Personality and Individual Differences* 51: 331–336.

Aubrey, A. 2019. "Anger Can Be Contagious—Here's How to Stop the Spread." *NPR Morning Edition*, February 19. https://www.npr.org/sections/health-shots/2019/02/25/697052006/anger-can-be-contagious-heres-how-to-stop-the-spread.

Barlow, D. H., T. J. Farchione, S. Sauer-Zavala, H. M. Latin, K. K. Ellard, J. R. Bullis, et al. 2017. *Unified Protocol for Transdiagnostic Treatment of Emotional Disorders: Therapist Guide.* 2nd ed. New York: Oxford University Press.

Buckingham, M. 2022. *Love and Work: How to Find What You Love, Love What You Do, and Do It for the Rest of Your Life.* Boston: Harvard Business Review Press.

Casey, B., S. Duhoux, and M. M. Cohen. 2010. "Adolescence: What Do Transmission, Transition, and Translation Have to Do with It?" *Neuron* 67: 749–760.

Clear, J. 2018. *Atomic Habits: An Easy and Proven Way to Build Good Habits and Break Bad Ones.* New York: Avery Publishing.

De Berardis, D., M. Fornaro, L. Orsolini, A. Ventriglio, F. Vellante, and M. Di Giannantonio. 2020. "Emotional Dysregulation in Adolescents: Implications for the Development of Severe Psychiatric Disorders, Substance Abuse, and Suicidal Ideation and Behaviors." *Brain Sciences* 10: 591.

Ekman, R., J. Giota, A. Eriksson, B. Thomas, and F. Bååthe. 2021. "A Flourishing Brain in the 21st Century: A Scoping Review of the Impact of Developing Good Habits for Mind, Brain, Well-Being, and Learning." *Mind, Brain, and Education* 16: 13–23.

Emmons, R. A. 2013. *Gratitude Works!: A 21-Day Program for Creating Emotional Prosperity.* San Francisco: Jossey-Bass.

Fernández-Berrocal, P., R. Alcaide, N. Extremera, and D. Pizarro. 2006. "The Role of Emotional Intelligence in Anxiety and Depression Among Adolescents." *Individual Differences Research* 4: 16–27.

Gillam, T. 2018. "Enhancing Public Mental Health and Wellbeing Through Creative Arts Participation." *Journal of Public Mental Health* 17(4): 148–156.

Hardy, J., and N. Zourbanos. 2016. "Self-Talk in Sport: Where Are We Now?" In *Routledge International Handbook of Sport Psychology*, 1st ed., edited by R. Schinke, K. R. McGannon, and B. Smith. London: Routledge.

Koelsch, S. 2018. "Investigating the Neural Encoding of Emotion with Music." *Neuron* 98(6): 1075–1079.

Laube, C., W. van den Bos, and Y. Fandakova. 2020. "The Relationship Between Pubertal Hormones and Brain Plasticity: Implications for Cognitive Training in Adolescence." *Developmental Cognitive Neuroscience* 42: 100753.

Littlefield, C. 2020. "Use Gratitude to Counter Stress and Uncertainty." *Harvard Business Review*, October 20. https://hbr.org/2020/10/use-gratitude-to-counter-stress-and-uncertainty.

Neff, K. 2023. "Exercise 5: Changing Your Critical Self-Talk." *Self-Compassion.* https://self-compassion.org/exercise-5-changing-critical-self-talk.

Nummenmaa, L., E. Glerean, R. Hari, and J. K. Hietanen. 2013. "Bodily Maps of Emotions." *Proceedings of the National Academy of Sciences* 111(2): 646–651.

Nummenmaa, L., R. Hari, J. K. Hietanen, and E. Glerean. 2018. "Maps of Subjective Feelings." *Proceedings of the National Academy of Sciences* 115(37): 9198–9203.

Parlamis, J. D. 2012. "Venting as Emotion Regulation: The Influence of Venting Responses and Respondent Identity on Anger and Emotional Tone." *International Journal of Conflict Management* 23(1): 77–96.

Pittman, C. M., and E. M. Karle. 2015. *Rewire Your Anxious Brain: How to Use the Neuroscience of Fear to End Anxiety, Panic, and Worry.* Oakland, CA: New Harbinger Publications.

Rideout, V., A. Peebles, S. Mann, and M. B. Robb. 2022. *Common Sense Census: Media Use by Tweens and Teens, 2021.* San Francisco: Common Sense. https://www.commonsensemedia.org/sites/default/files/research/report/8-18-census-integrated-report-final-web_0.pdf.

Russell, J. A. 1980. "A Circumplex Model of Affect." *Journal of Personality and Social Psychology* 39(6): 1161–1178.

Salovey, P., A. Woolery, L. Stroud, and E. Epel. 2002. "Perceived Emotional Intelligence, Stress Reactivity, and Symptom Reports: Further Explorations Using the Trait Meta-Mood Scale." *Psychology and Health* 17(5): 611–627.

Santos-Rosa, F. J., C. Montero-Carretero, L. A. Gómez-Landero, M. Torregrossa, and E. Cervelló. 2022. "Positive and Negative Spontaneous Self-Talk and Performance in Gymnastics: The Role of Contextual, Personal and Situational Factors." *PLoS One* 17(3): e0265809.

Staras, K., H.-S. Chang, and M. P. Gilbey. 2001. "Resetting of Sympathetic Rhythm by Somatic Afferents Causes Post-Reflex Coordination of Sympathetic Activity in Rat." *Journal of Physiology* 533(2): 537–545.

Suttie, J. 2021. "Does Venting Your Feelings Actually Help?" *Greater Good Magazine*, June 21. https://greatergood.berkeley.edu/article/item/does _venting_your_feelings_actually_help.

Tseng, J., and J. Poppenk. 2020. "Brain Meta-State Transitions Demarcate Thoughts Across Task Contexts Exposing the Mental Noise of Trait Neuroticism." *Nature Communications* 11: 3480.

Weir, K. 2020. "Nurtured by Nature." *American Psychological Association Monitor on Psychology* 51(3): 50.

Willcox, G. 1982. "The Feeling Wheel: A Tool for Expanding Awareness of Emotions and Increasing Spontaneity and Intimacy." *Transactional Analysis Journal* 12(4): 274–276.

Yarwood, M. 2022. *Psychology of Human Emotion: An Open Access Textbook.* Pressbooks, Pennsylvania State University. https://psu.pb.unizin.org/psych 425/chapter/circumplex-models.

Young K. S., C. F. Sandman, and M. G. Craske. 2019. "Positive and Negative Emotion Regulation in Adolescence: Links to Anxiety and Depression." *Brain Science* 9(4): 76.

Melanie McNally, PsyD, is a licensed clinical psychologist and brain coach who helps tweens, teens, and young adults become the superheroes of their life stories. She is a strong advocate for teen mental health, and was a White House panelist where she spoke about youth mental health needs. She is founder of Destination You, a place where tweens, teens, young adults, and their parents get support through virtual coaching, teletherapy, virtual groups, self-guided programs, and other resources.

More ⏱Instant Help Books for Teens

An Imprint of New Harbinger Publications

THE ACTION MINDSET WORKBOOK FOR TEENS

Simple CBT Skills to Help You Conquer Fear and Self-Doubt and Take Steps Toward What Really Matters

978-1648480461 / US $18.95

HEALING RACIAL STRESS WORKBOOK FOR BLACK TEENS

Skills to Help You Manage Emotions, Resist Racism, and Feel Empowered

978-1648480676 / US $17.95

CONQUER NEGATIVE THINKING FOR TEENS

A Workbook to Break the Nine Thought Habits That Are Holding You Back

978-1626258891 / US $17.95

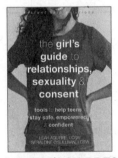

THE GIRL'S GUIDE TO RELATIONSHIPS, SEXUALITY, AND CONSENT

Tools to Help Teens Stay Safe, Empowered, and Confident

978-1684039739 / US $19.95

PUT YOUR WORRIES HERE

A Creative Journal for Teens with Anxiety

978-1684032143 / US $18.95

JUST AS YOU ARE

A Teen's Guide to Self-Acceptance and Lasting Self-Esteem

978-1626255906 / US $17.95

🌱 **newharbinger**publications

1-800-748-6273 / newharbinger.com

(VISA, MC, AMEX / prices subject to change without notice)   Follow Us 📷 f 🐦 ▶ 📌 in

Don't miss out on new books from New Harbinger.
Subscribe to our email list at **newharbinger.com/subscribe** 🖱